when the
seagulls follow
the trawler

when the seagulls follow the trawler

football in the 90s

tom whitworth

First published by Pitch Publishing, 2021

Pitch Publishing
A2 Yeoman Gate
Yeoman Way
Worthing
Sussex
BN13 3QZ
www.pitchpublishing.co.uk
info@pitchpublishing.co.uk

ISBN 978 1 78531 761 3

Typesetting and origination by Pitch Publishing
Printed and bound in India by Replika Press Pvt. Ltd.

Contents

Prologue: There We Were 7

1. In Manchester – Part I 17

2. Dancing in the Streets. 47

3. Our Friends in the North 59

4. A Stadium for the 90s 88

5. Football's Coming Home 106

6. The Flickering Flame 122

7. Revolution 166

8. In Manchester – Part II 199

Epilogue: Here We Are. 235

Acknowledgements 241

Bibliography 243

Prologue

There We Were

THEY SAY you shouldn't look back. That to dwell on the past for too long does you no good. Always move forward. Reflect, then move on. But remember the 90s?

In Britain it was a decade of optimism and change, vibrancy and brightness, opportunity and emergence. A new way forward after the slog of the Margaret Thatcher 80s. It as when people listened to the 'Britpop' bands like Oasis and voted into power Tony Blair's New Labour project. When they built the Channel Tunnel and made TV programmes like *The Fast Show*. When people drank those little cartons of Capri-Sun and Chris Evans, Gaby Roslin, and Zig and Zag started off your day on *The Big Breakfast*. It was when Ewan McGregor's Renton character ran around Edinburgh to an Iggy Pop tune in Danny Boyle's 1996 film *Trainspotting*, declaring 'Choose life … Choose a career … Choose a fucking big television.' And when they put up those traffic-stopping 'Hello Boys' Wonderbra billboards. So here's to looking back.

In the important world of football, changes were coming along too as the game moved into its own brighter future, away from the volatility and danger of the 70s and 80s to a new era of sanitised supporter experience and inclusivity. The 1990s – the decade when football emerged from its slumber, progressed and took its place in the mainstream of popular British culture.

On the pitch there would be tactical evolution as teams caught up with their European neighbours. The number of players and managers brought in from abroad would increase every year and there would be the shift from widespread booze culture to a more continental temperance approach, with pasta. On the muddying and bobbly playing surfaces, memorable moments were plentiful and goals would be scored by Robbie Fowler, Matt Le Tissier, Dennis Bergkamp, Roberto Baggio and, in off the crossbar, Tony Yeboah. The birth of the new Premier League, with the 'It's a whole new ball game' Sky Sports advert, would lead to a bonanza of ever-spiralling transfer fees and player wages. Satellite television would beam the games into the pubs and living rooms of the fans. The standing terraces would make way for all-seater stands and many would be priced out of the newly transformed grounds.

The players even looked different. As one friend pointed out to me, the 1980s footballer seemed to have black hair and a moustache and wore short shorts. By the 90s the moustaches would mostly be gone and the kits would be baggier, featuring bolder and brasher shades and patterns. Plastered across them would be the club sponsors: mobile-phone networks, electronics manufacturers and lager brands.

The 1990s – when the game and its image moved out of the dark and into the light. When its image shifted from black and white to colour. Football's very own transition from 'Old' to 'New'.

I grew up in the 90s so it was my decade of footballing enlightenment, when I'd been taken along to the matches and had seen for the first time the vast green expanse of the pitches. I had watched and listened to the fans in the stands singing and shouting, and heard the swearing blokes around me. I had my first kits bought for me, home and away (thanks Mum and Dad), and collected Merlin Premier League stickers – my 'swaps' kept together by an elastic band for trading at school. I played *Championship Manager* on the family PC for far too many hours and for a few seasons was able to learn the name of nearly every Premier League player, along with the position they played. I watched the build-up to the FA Cup Finals that began hours before kick-off, recording them on our VHS player and neatly labelling them with the stickers those blank Scotch tapes came with. Until we got Sky Sports in our house, I'd walk round excitedly to friends' homes to watch the games.

Back in 1992, my club Sheffield Wednesday were founder members of the Premier League. But by the year 2000 they would be relegated from it. A few years ago I wrote a book called *Owls*, about their decline and subsequent wilderness. I opened some doors, spoke to many people and learned a lot about my club. Then I put down the words, 70,000 or so. Today as I type, 20 years and counting since Wednesday's drop from the top division, any kind of return for them seems a fair way off. The emergence of the Premier League and the revolutions that came to the game through the 90s seemed to take place away from my club as they drifted. As football transitioned from 'Old' to 'New', Wednesday did not.

What, then, happened to football around the rest of the country during this time? What changed and where did it happen? Who lived through it and what did they experience? I decided to get out there and talk to the fans and the players, the owners and the managers who were there. I'd go to the towns and the cities that their clubs call home: Manchester, Newcastle and Huddersfield; Liverpool and north London. Following the narrative of a football year, the 2017/18 football season, I'd visit the stadiums, sit in pubs and cafes, read the books and watch the old footage. I'd let the Dictaphone run and run, unpick the past then write it up.

* * * *

For many people in Britain, the 1980s had been a decade of political and social bleakness. A time when things seemed broken and wrong. 1979 had seen Thatcher's election as Conservative Prime Minister and what followed under her leadership proved catastrophic to the lives and livelihoods of millions of people up and down the country. The union movement was crushed, the industries and communities that were built around them decimated, unemployment reached three million. Still, the 'Iron Lady' was re-elected in 1983 and again in 1987 to prolong her controversial reign.

In football, meanwhile, it had been a time of violence, tragedy and decline during which the image of the nation's game lay firmly in the gutter. Despite the achievements of Nottingham Forest, Aston Villa and Liverpool on the European stage (from 1977–82 they won the European Cup every season, three times in Liverpool's case and twice in Forest's), football had big problems. By the 1985/86 season, total Football League attendances had dipped to the lowest on record at 16.4 million (the previous decade the figure had been around ten million higher). Hooliganism was widespread and out of control. In 1985 Luton and Millwall rioted at Kenilworth Road, while in the Midlands one fan had died as Birmingham City and Leeds United hooligans clashed violently at St Andrew's. The grounds were crumbling and in some cases were tragically unsafe. As one damning piece in the *Sunday Times* would comment around the time, football was 'a slum sport played in slum stadiums increasingly watched by slum people'.

May 1985 had seen a fire blaze through an old wooden stand at Bradford City's Valley Parade ground that killed 56 people. Years of debris that had accumulated underneath the stand had caught alight and it had taken only minutes for the fire to rage through. That same month at the dilapidated Heysel Stadium in Brussels, 39 Juventus supporters were killed before the European Cup Final against Liverpool after a wall collapsed following a rush from the Liverpool section. After Heysel, all English clubs were banned from European competition for five years and Liverpool for six.

Then came the darkest day, in 1989, at an FA Cup semi-final in Sheffield, which resulted in 96 football fans losing their lives after they themselves were crushed in the dangerous and overcrowded 'pens' of Hillsborough's Leppings Lane terrace. In the shameful aftermath, the Liverpool supporters were falsely accused of being drunken, ticketless hooligans who were responsible for the disaster. The findings of a subsequent two-year inquest into the disaster laid out the reality, however: culpability lay in the hands of the South Yorkshire Police, Sheffield Wednesday Football Club and Sheffield City Council.

The game was plumbing the depths and things had to change. In 1990, the year after the fall of the Berlin Wall, the FIFA World Cup took place in Italy (the country that was home to the best football league in the world, Serie A). Italy had the most money, much of which came from wealthy benefactor owners like Silvio Berlusconi of AC Milan and the Agnelli family of Juventus. It had the most astute coaches, like Giovanni Trapattoni at Inter and Arrigo Sacchi at AC Milan, plus the world's greatest players – an eclectic mix of technically gifted Italians and expensively imported overseas stars: Roberto Baggio, Franco Baresi, Roberto Mancini and Gianluca Vialli, Diego Maradona, Ruud Gullit, Frank Rijkaard and Marco van Basten.

England's David Platt would later move over from Aston Villa, firstly to Bari then on to Juventus and Sampdoria. Platt loved Italy's food and the weather and how he could 'call in at the local bar in the mornings on my way in to work to read the papers, drink coffee and chat with the locals'. In 1992, Nottingham Forest's Des Walker would follow him over, too, moving to Sampdoria, as would the genius footballing talent Paul 'Gazza' Gascoigne after his £5.5m transfer from Tottenham to Lazio (sadly, though, Gascoigne's time in Rome would be hindered by injuries).

The 1990 World Cup had as its backdrop Italy's glamorous cities and their epic stadiums: the grand San Siro in Milan, with its spiral concrete walkways; the Stadio Olimpico in Rome; in Turin, the brand new Delle Alpi that sat beside the Italian Alps. For its soundtrack, the tournament had Luciano Pavarotti's rousing performance of 'Nessun Dorma'.

Thanks to the progress made by Bobby Robson's England side through the rounds (they were soundtracked by New Order's 'World in Motion'), interest in the game had re-ignited back home. Although the tournament delivered fairly defensive football and on average the lowest number of goals per match (2.2) for any finals to that point, as Gary Lineker, Chris Waddle and Gascoigne made their way to the semi-finals and a showdown with West Germany in Turin, back home in England excitement grew and grew. Some 25 million watched the Germany game on TV and saw Gazza's yellow card (which would have ruled him out of the final had England progressed) and his famous tears, and they watched the penalty shoot-out misses from Stuart Pearce and Waddle that sent England on their way. Despite the defeat, the players returned home heroes and enthusiasm exploded for the domestic season ahead.

In 1989/90 Liverpool won the First Division title, then Arsenal in '1990/91 and Leeds United the following year. Across the leagues, attendances were rising.

In late 1990, Margaret Thatcher's 11-year reign as prime minister had come to an end, her party turning on her and ousting her from power, with John Major taking her place. The country was suffering through a recession and September 1992 saw the collapse of the pound on 'Black Wednesday' when Britain left the European Exchange Rate Mechanism. Interest rates hit 15 per cent and earlier in the year the Maastricht Treaty had been signed to rebrand the European Community (formerly the European Economic Community) as the European Union, of which Britain was still a part.

* * * *

The 1992/93 season saw the arrival of the Premier League, the new and long-planned English football super league. The big moment had come back in 1991 when it was announced that a top-level breakaway division would be formed. Pushed by the 'Big Five' clubs of the time – Liverpool, Everton, Manchester United, Tottenham and Arsenal – the league would sit separate from the Football League (which would continue to run the three divisions below).

The Premier League would kick off with a five-year £304m broadcasting deal (dwarfing the previous £44m four-season arrangement) and bring Sunday afternoon and Monday evening games to satellite television. There were glossier and more in-your-face graphics and coverage, fireworks and bright suits and groovy ties worn by Sky Sports presenter Richard Keys. Tactical analysis came from former Everton striker Andy Gray and there were dancers for the crowds. Larger clubs were to be quids-in since they received bigger slices of the top flight's growing broadcasting revenues. These new-found riches would be spent on players – specifically, their transfer fees and wages. The most money paid out by an English club in 1992/93 was the £3.6m spent by Blackburn Rovers on Southampton striker Alan Shearer. By the end of the decade, Shearer's subsequent £15m move to Newcastle in 1996 would be the biggest. In that first Premier League season, a top division footballer in England earned on average just under £1,500 per week. In the mid-80s, this had been less than £500 per week. By 1999/2000, the average was over £7,000, with the top players earning far more than that.

Over time, the Premier League would become the richest league in the world. Its second broadcasting deal, covering the four seasons between 1997/98 and 2000/01, would come in at £670m, more than double the first £304m deal. And thanks to the transformative influence of players and managers imported from abroad, the league would emerge as one of, if not the most, entertaining and best in the world. Simultaneously, the rising cost of tickets for the matches would extend beyond the means of many supporters whose loyalties would be tested to the limit. In 1990, the average ticket price for top-division football had been £5; in 1993 it would rise to almost £9. By 1999, over £16. Premier League grounds would still be packed, though, with annual attendances of 9.7m in 1992/93 increasing to 11.6m by 1999/2000.

The first televised Sky game of 1992/93 came at the City Ground, Nottingham, where Brian Clough's Forest side took on Graeme Souness's Liverpool. Despite a 2-1 win for the hosts, Clough's team would be poor throughout the season, spending most of it in the bottom places in the table before eventually getting relegated. Sadly at the time Clough's blotchy face betrayed the alcoholism that was undermining the talents of the legendary manager. Twice that season he had stuck his two fingers up to a jeering Forest crowd and gone were the glory days of his back-to-back European Cup wins for the club in 1979 and 19'80.

In an interview he gave that year, Clough would say of his Forest side, 'I'm telling you, we've been absolute, total shit for most of this season.' Then, reflecting on what was happening around him in football at the time, he said, 'I'm getting older, the players are getting younger … the game is moving on.'

1

In Manchester – Part I

Off Their Perch

By the time Alex Ferguson's Manchester United visited Carrow Road to face Norwich City in early April 1993, they sat third in the Premier League table, two points behind their hosts and four behind Aston Villa who were leading them all. That evening, the performance United gave in front of the Sky cameras for *Monday Night Football* was breathtakingly devastating, clinical and winning – all that was good about the side that Ferguson had built.

In their green-and-yellow change strip, a nod to the club's Newton Heath origins, they destroyed Norwich in the first 21 minutes of the game, blowing them away with three superb, counter-attacking goals. Ryan Giggs opened the scoring, Andrei Kanchelskis made it 2-0, and then, after Paul Ince had intercepted the ball inside his own half, the midfielder charged forward and played it across the box to their French maestro forward Eric Cantona for 3-0. 'United were fantastic that night,' says fan Andy Walsh from the comfort of his living room in his neat semi-detached Stretford house. 'Really blistering. There was a swagger about them that night. They were just on another planet.'

United were searching for their first title since 1967 – too long for a club of their size and stature – and the iconic moment of the run-in came the following Saturday at home to Sheffield Wednesday. Trailing by a goal with only minutes left in the game, defender Steve Bruce rose to head in the equaliser before, deep into injury time, doing the same for the winner. On the sidelines Ferguson celebrated joyfully, his arms in the air, and his assistant Brian Kidd leapt around on the pitch. The win put United top of the table.

'I don't actually remember much about the match apart from just completely losing it when Bruce's second goal went in,' recalls Walsh. 'It was a very emotional moment, like an out-of-body experience. Being in the ground with my dad and the lads that I'd gone to school with, and experienced so much with over the past 20-odd years made it even more special. I was so emotional that day; I can feel it now just talking about it.'

After that win United picked up maximum points on the run-in, striding on to take the title and become the first Premier League champions. 'After we won it, we went into town and stayed out on the piss for two days,' says Walsh. 'I don't remember much more than that really.'

* * * *

The winding Snake Pass road that links over to Glossop then Manchester starts somewhere at the top of Sheffield. It takes you all the way up into the peaks before the eventual descent on the other side. Today it is clear and bright and the scenery is beautiful as I make my way over the hills to Stretford, Manchester.

Andy Walsh is a passionate and thoughtful guy who speaks with the strong Manchester twang. I used to live over here and listening to him talk is a familiar and comforting sound. Now with grey hair and glasses, Walsh first saw United in person when he was five, standing with his father on the cigarette-smoky terraces of Old Trafford at the end of the 1960s. He became a regular, a season ticket holder, watching the Reds every other week. For me, he is the everyman football supporter: passionate and devoted.

'Going to United was just something our family did,' he says. 'My dad used to go with his brother and his mates and I can remember pestering him on a Saturday for me to go with him. When he did take me it was special – the atmosphere and the banter and the game – it was great. The sense of being part of a big crowd had a huge impact on me.'

When he was older, Walsh went to the games with his school-mates, 'From probably about the age of ten or 11, we were going on our own. We'd queue up outside the ground for ages, get through the turnstiles, then leg it up the different stairways to try and get our spot in the ground early.

'We all had paper rounds and jobs on milk floats, working in local shops and things like that, just to get the money together for the game. I lost a couple of jobs because, you know, there might be a game on that day and you wanted to go to that instead of working. I remember having a difficult conversation with a local greengrocer once when I just didn't understand why he couldn't let me off on a Saturday when United were at home. That job lasted about two weeks.'

As the years went by a routine developed. 'We'd be under the stand drinking and singing, dancing and bouncing around,' remembers Walsh. 'It was just brilliant, absolutely mental.' The lads were growing up together, got 'proper' jobs on building sites, as office clerks, a couple were musicians. 'I was in a bank,' says Walsh. As money allowed, they'd follow United to away games up and down the country, having a laugh and drinking beer all day, some of them jibbing into the grounds.

Walsh's journey around Old Trafford would take him from the Stretford Paddock and the Scoreboard Paddock, round to the United Road Stand opposite the dugouts, then K Stand behind the goal. The areas were cheap – milk- and paper-round fare – and were filled with lively younger lads (around the time Walsh started going to the games the average age of fans on the 'Stretty' was 18). Notable from the videos of United's early-1990s seasons are those kind of lads in the crowd, jumping up and down wildly when goals were scored – all joyous and uninhibited.

Walsh lives in Stretford partly because it is where he grew up but partly because he wanted to be nearer to United. 'It's the second house we've had here. The one before was 500 yards closer to Old Trafford,' he says. The drive here from the ground takes five minutes.

In the 90s he became involved in IMUSA (Independent Manchester United Supporters' Association), a group that became active in club matters affecting the fans such as ticket pricing. I had known about Walsh for some of the activities he had been involved in over the years, particularly his activism for United. Later on in the 90s, he and others fought back against a major takeover of United that in his eyes threatened the fabric of the club he loved – he wrote a book about it. Back in 1991, he was jailed for 14 days for refusing to pay the unpopular and riot-provoking new poll tax. 'I was adamantly against it and was eventually jailed for non-payment,' he says. 'A warrant had been issued for my arrest and United were actually playing in Rotterdam in the Cup Winners' Cup Final [1991], so I decided that leaving the country wasn't the right thing to do. But I still disappeared for a couple of days, so I could watch the game. I just didn't go home and slept at a mate's house, then handed myself in at Stretford nick.'

As United got closer to the title in 1992/93, Walsh had in the back of his mind events from the previous season. With five games to go, United had sat two points clear at the top of the First Division table. In the team they'd had the excellent Peter Schmeichel in goal, the solid Steve Bruce and Gary Pallister at the back, Bryan Robson and Ince bossing the centre of midfield, Andrei Kanchelskis and the skilful youngster Ryan Giggs on the wings, with Mark Hughes getting the goals up front. That season the title was at last within United's reach. Stay the course and win it – that was all that was needed. But then they blew it, lost three times in the final stages and handed the crown to Leeds United.

'A lot of us got swept up in thinking it was going to happen that year,' remembers Walsh of United's late collapse that season. 'We *were* going to win the title. I was convinced. Then I went on holiday, which I never used to do before the end of the season. Then naturally when we lost it I blamed myself. I remember thinking that we'd lost it because I'd gone away. As a football fan all rationality goes out of the window with that kind of thing. But I really had thought we were going to do it that year. I still think I'm partly to blame for going away and not seeing the season out.'

A year later, as 1992/93 drew to a close, Walsh didn't go on holiday and this time he was around to catch the run-in and enjoy the celebrations. He and his friends and family, the people with whom he'd shared so many memories and experiences of watching United, celebrated in style, savouring every moment. United's 26-year wait for the league was over.

* * * *

If there is one football club that best represents the journey of English football in the 1990s, it is Manchester United. Throughout this era of great change for the game that saw the formation of the breakaway Premier League and its emergence, United were at the centre of both English football's commercial rise and the development of its clubs as globalised mega-brands, along with their gradual revival in European competition.

In the dark Thatcher 80s Liverpool had been the dominant force in English football, but in the 90s it was Ferguson's dynamic team that would be all-conquering, lifting five of the first seven Premier League titles. Old Trafford would grow to become the largest club ground in the country. Shares in the plc company which owned the football club and paid the ballooning player wages and transfer fees of the time could be freely bought and sold. And the United brand would become one of the most popular and coveted in world sport. In Manchester, England, it truly was 'a whole new ball game'.

In Manchester. Beside the Pennine hills where the city's Industrial Revolution mills had turned 'Cottonopolis' into one of the wealthiest cities in the world. Where in 1894 they had built a vast inland port and ship canal because they wanted one. Where in 1917 they had split the atom. Where by the 1980s the bands Joy Division then New Order emerged from the renowned Factory Records label. And where by the 1990s gang-related gun crime was a blight for the city's reputation, earning it the nickname 'Gunchester'.

Alex Ferguson moved here from Aberdeen in November 1986 after he had won three league titles, four Scottish cups and the European Cup Winners' Cup for the Dons. His ability to compete with the bigger and wealthier Old Firm clubs of Glasgow, coupled with his reputation as an ambitious and strong-willed workaholic manager, had earned him many admirers in England. Some 19 years after United's previous league title success, the club's hierarchy believed he could be the man to return them to the top – or in his own words, to knock dominant Liverpool 'right off their fucking perch'.

Andy Walsh had been impressed with Ferguson when he had arrived at the club, particularly when it came to what he stood for and how he came across. He says, 'I liked him straight away. He knew what United were about and what was important. He had this willingness to learn about the club from all angles, too. He had this desire to get under the skin of the club and understand its history. Talking authoritatively about its history and its players, his respect for Matt Busby and the players from the past. All of that was very different from what had gone before.

'One of the things that struck me as well was his personal politics: [he was] a trade unionist and self-declared socialist. I thought this guy has a set of values that you don't usually come across in football.

'He also had this great ability to connect with the fans from day one. The efforts that he made to speak to supporters; the stories you heard of people bumping into him outside bars and restaurants in town, where he stopped and had time for them. He would stand and talk to people and made himself available. To me that was really quite important.

'He created that sense of club and he was insistent on the players understanding United and its history. He made sure that his dressing room, whether that be players, coaching staff or support staff – people in the kit room, the people who did the tea – interacted with the supporters properly. That was positive, I thought.'

The transformation under Ferguson would not come quickly. He had inherited a squad with problems, specifically a drinking culture. Individuals that were said to be at the core of this, such as Paul McGrath and Norman Whiteside, would be moved on. Organisation and investment were needed for the youth set-up, too, along generally with greater discipline throughout the club. Several troubled seasons would have to be steered through as performances often failed to meet expectations – while second place in the First Division in 1987/88 was encouraging, 11th the following year was not. Average crowds at Old Trafford had dipped below 40,000.

There was some success. The FA Cup was lifted in 1990 and the European Cup Winners' Cup a year later. They came close to that title in 1991/92, before Andy Walsh went on holiday and United lost their nerve and blew it to make it 25 years and counting since their last top-flight championship.

A stuttering start to 1992/93 had given little encouragement: two defeats and one draw from their opening three games. By early November they sat tenth in the table and in the seven games leading up to that point had scored just four times without winning. Ferguson's United needed something different, something better. A big bang.

Forty miles away in Leeds they had it – something different, something better. An influential forward who in 1991/92 had helped spur Howard Wilkinson's side to the First Division title at United's expense. A maverick and a transformer. A Frenchman.

* * * *

Up until that point Eric Cantona had lived out a nomadic existence in French football, regularly falling out with people and getting banned, and briefly retiring from the game in exasperation at his treatment. He could be broody and difficult but, as English football would come to learn, he was also a supreme player and a unique and entertaining character.

Powerful and confident on the pitch, with an elegance and intelligence as both a goal-maker and goal-scorer Cantona played with his head up and back straight, his chest puffed out. One of his managers astutely observed how he mainly looked for the simplest and most effective pass, only playing the extravagant ball when necessary. Off the pitch, he liked art and on team nights out drank champagne while others downed beers.

Statistically, his impact on Leeds's championship side had been modest – three goals in 15 games since joining from French side Nimes. Leeds won only one of the five matches he had started before the 1991/92 title was won.

What he did bring to the table, though, was something different, a vital coolness and an unmistakeable charisma. As one of his team-mates at Leeds, Gary McAllister would explain, 'When it came to winning the championship, Eric played a pivotal part ... [he] would come on when we struggled to find a way through ... get the crowd going with a little bit of magic ... the crowd would lift us ... [then] we'd score an important goal.'

How Cantona came to be at Old Trafford is a pivotal 1990s football story. In short, after Leeds had first enquired about signing United's full-back Denis Irwin only to be told they had no chance, their rivals from Manchester then enquired about Cantona. Leeds were open to a sale and for just £1m United were able to get their man. Howard Wilkinson thought the Yorkshire club were better off with the cash rather than their continental verve and the Leeds fans had to cry into their beers. Alex Ferguson would describe the deal as 'an absolute steal'.

'At first I wasn't that excited about him coming to us to be honest,' remembers Walsh of United's new signing. 'In my circle of mates it was like, "He's never done anything special against us, so what?" I guess the fact that the Leeds fans were pissed off was a plus.

'But then you started to see him play and it was like, "Fuckin' 'ell! OK, I'm going with this. This is exciting. This guy's cut from a different cloth."'

The impact that Cantona was to have on his new team would be completely transformational. Deployed off Mark Hughes in the United attack, his imagination and ability to find space and time brought a brilliant new creative dimension to United. Club legend George Best would note how Cantona had 'given this team a brain'. They opened up and the quality of the rest of the group shone through even more as their confidence grew. In the nine league games that followed his debut in late 1992, they won six times, drew twice, lost once and scored 22 goals as they worked their way to the top of the table.

'As time went by the admiration for Eric grew,' explains Walsh. 'It wasn't instant but it grew. That wasn't just because of what he was doing on the pitch. One thing I liked about him, something that we learnt when we heard his interviews, was how there was that sense of the supporter in him. You felt like he was doing it for you. You felt like he cared and from pretty early on you could see that.'

As Cantona would say of his role as a footballer, 'So much the better if my goals give you something to sing about. Nothing else is important.'

As Walsh says, 'He cared about his performance. He cared about his team-mates' performance, the team's performance and the result. He cared about the *way* they won. All the things that you cared about as a supporter were embodied in this bloke and that was absolutely intoxicating. It made you proud to be a United fan.'

The new man appeared to be United's final piece in the jigsaw. Old Trafford was buzzing – buzzing for Cantona – and after those key victories over Norwich and Sheffield Wednesday in 1993 they ran on to pick up the title by ten points.

* * * *

When his United players reported for pre-season training before the 1993/94 season, Ferguson asked them whether they were hungry for more success. As they went on to win

13 of their opening 15 games, playing fast and thrilling football a notch up even from the impressiveness of the previous campaign, there was no doubt that they still were. By the end of the season the Premier League would be comfortably retained and the FA Cup was lifted too, completing the domestic Double.

This was the season that Cantona really emerged as the main star at Old Trafford, scoring 25 goals in all competitions and creating 15 for others. Among them was a match-winning free kick against Arsenal at Old Trafford, plus the two strikes that orchestrated a comeback victory at Manchester City. During an FA Cup tie at Wimbledon, despite being kicked around by their basic midfielder Vinnie Jones for much of the afternoon, Cantona repeatedly got up, carried on and went on to score another wonderful goal – a volley teed up and blasted into the corner of the net. By now, the United supporters were in true unwavering awe of the man who wore the collar of his shirt up and for whom at Christmas they sang their chant 'The 12 Days of Cantona'. The man they called 'King Eric'.

Cantona was similarly impressive off the pitch, never acting the Big Time Charlie or playing up to the role of the celebrity that he undoubtedly was. In the city he could be seen playing table football in pubs like the cosy Peveril of the Peak or visiting the Cornerhouse arthouse cinema.

'I think he was genuine and realised that he had a role with people,' says Walsh. 'That he was important in other peoples' lives. He understood that position and he always had time for them. There are stories about him not leaving the car park at the training ground until everyone who wanted a photo had got one, or everyone who wanted something signing got it signed. That kind of thing was important. It wasn't PR or spin. It wasn't plastic or kissing the badge bollocks. It was all genuine.'

In the end United took the 1993/94 title with 92 points, eight clear of their nearest rivals Blackburn Rovers, the provincial Lancashire club who were funded by the steel millionaire Jack Walker, managed by Kenny Dalglish and saw most of their goals scored by their £3.6m striker Alan Shearer. Ferguson's men had led the table since August and never shifted from there all season. After the league was secured, they went on to beat Chelsea 4-0 in the FA Cup Final at Wembley. Cantona, of course, calmly slotted away two penalties.

Man Utd Plc

Coinciding with the rise of the United team though the 1990s was their surge into footballing financial super-dominance. By 1991 Manchester United was valued at £47m, its emergence as a commercial vehicle and international brand that sold millions of pounds of merchandising to its fans around the globe in full swing. This was set to continue right through the decade and beyond. By 1998, a buyer would need over £500m to buy the club, which at the time of writing is now worth just under £3bn.

Back in 1980, the 35-year old Martin Edwards had taken over as United chairman after inheriting a controlling stake from his father Louis, a wealthy local butcher. It was under Edwards junior that the commercial transformation of the club would gather pace. In 1986, he had appointed Alex Ferguson as manager before later hiring a man named Edward Freedman as head of merchandising. While the former would take care of the football, the latter looked after the United brand – the main manifestation of

Freeman's work coming in December 1994 when the club's megastore opened at the ground. On matchdays, supporters could now be seen clutching carrier bags of logo-featuring merchandise, while thousands would be seen wearing the latest team strip (United changed theirs regularly around this period, having at times three different strips each season – one home and two changes). Old Trafford also had a museum that welcomed over 100,000 visitors a year. With fans visiting even on non-matchdays, the ground was a seven-days-a-week cash register. 'If you like money, Old Trafford is a great place to be,' the United fan and journalist Jim White wrote in 1994.

Before meeting Andy Walsh, I had parked up near Old Trafford and walked around the gigantic stands. Inside, the 74,000 seats are accessed by the nod-to-the-past red wooden turnstile doors. The Sir Alex Ferguson Stand (his knighthood would come in 1999) is almost guarded by his bronze statue that stands outside with arms folded. There's the shop, where branded golf balls, bottle-openers and replica kits are for sale. And there are more statues: Sir Matt Busby, Georgie Best, Denis Law and Bobby Charlton. It wasn't a matchday when I was there but a good number of fans were milling around, taking photos and buying stuff.

In 1991, Edwards took the major step of moving the club to a stock-market listing. This now meant that the plc that owned the club had as its primary objective to grow profits, increasing its market value and paying out dividends to its shareholders. Shares could be freely bought and sold by investors and with enough of these, any single party – such as a global media organisation or a wealthy overseas investor (which might not support the club but might like the idea of its profits) – could feasibly make a full takeover bid. At the time of the flotation Alex Ferguson was not in favour of the idea and supposedly refused to take up his entitlement of shares. 'My own feeling is that the club is too important as a sporting institution, too much of a rarity, to be put up for sale,' he would say.

'Personally, at the time, I saw a share issue itself for what it was,' explains Walsh. 'It was a way of raising funds for the club, the company. The bigger shareholders would still have influence but there was a large number of United fans who saw it as a method to get a platform at the club, having been ignored before on a number of issues that had previously been pushed to one side and dismissed. So people saw this as an opportunity to get a stake in the club, to go to meetings and hold the club to account. A couple of people in my circle saw it as an opportunity to ask questions at shareholders' meetings.'

When the flotation went ahead, £6.7m was initially raised towards the construction of the new Stretford End stand.

* * * *

Traditionally, the cheap terraces on Old Trafford's Stretford End had been where the more youthful element of United's support stood for games, helping to create the lively atmosphere of a matchday in the packed and vibrant stand. At the end of the 1991/92 season, it was flattened to make way for its 10,164-seated £10.3m replacement which was completed the following summer. This marked the first stage of the ground's redevelopment and would be followed by the conversion of the Scoreboard End to all-seater (Lord Justice Taylor's post-Hillsborough report into the 1989 disaster had determined that at the top levels of the game in England and Scotland the standing terraces had to make way for seats). Later, the construction of the three-tier, £20m, 25,000-capacity North Stand would take Old Trafford's total capacity to 55,000. Following the transition from standing to seating, many would point to a shift in the atmosphere at Old Trafford. It was a safer and a nicer experience, but for many the atmosphere was diminished, with less singing and much less raucousness. It was a similar story across the country as clubs converted or reconstructed their grounds.

Developments also brought in new corporate areas that included glassed-off executive boxes and large hospitality suites. When Old Trafford's capacity reached 55,000 seats, 2,000 would be reserved for corporate guests or sponsors. For many, this was a further detriment to atmosphere. Paul Parker, a player in Ferguson's early 1990s teams, would later note a drop off in atmosphere during his time playing for the club. 'I noticed it in my second season when the Stretford End wasn't there and it got worse over the years … too many corporate fans who are more concerned about being in Old Trafford than supporting the team.'

'That was the culture around the game at the time,' says Walsh. 'You definitely got a sense that the suits in the boardroom saw everything as a marketing exercise. United was a bit of a hothouse for all of the commercial things that were happening because of their size and their pursuit of the corporate dollar. It really was becoming a corporate juggernaut and the plc was very much seen as being something that was outside of the club. An atmosphere developed amongst many of the fans of "Love the club, hate the 'business'." It wasn't just the corporate hospitality and things like that which some of the fans had a problem with, it was the commercialisation of what was ours – our football club.

'Another big thing that was happening at this time was the increase in the number of games picked for television. Kick-off times and dates were moved and for me that was part of a slow destruction of the matchday experience. Shifting fixtures for television meant you then had to shift your life around. You didn't know what time you were kicking off at: 12.30pm, 3pm, 5.30pm? Or what day: Saturday, Sunday, Monday? It was a nightmare and it started to affect your matchday routine. Even if you could make it to a game, the people that you went with might not have been able to.'

To many match-going supporters at the time, most concerning was the rising cost of tickets. While buying a replica kit or sitting in the corporate hospitality seats at Old Trafford were matters of choice, less so was paying over your money to pass through the turnstile to watch the team you loved. In 1991/92, a season ticket at Old Trafford for standing on K Stand cost £110.50. By 1994/95, a season ticket there (now for a seat) had risen to £266. Nationally, the average price of a ticket for a top-flight match was around £11.50 that year.

'In reality loads of our fans couldn't care less about how many shirts the club brought out or what the latest tacky merchandise was being pushed through the megastore,' explains Walsh, 'Ryan Giggs duvets or whatever. But what was important were the ticket prices. Please keep the ticket prices down because if you're a football fan, you've not really got a choice about going to a game. I accept that they could have filled Old Trafford three or four times over for every match, but it was about accessibility for fans. I think they just saw it a supply and demand equation rather than a cultural issue. The team was really flying, winning trophies and playing brilliant football. But at the same time this commercialisation was happening and for me that was becoming a problem.

'During that time the football was brilliant; going to games was fantastic. You could still go without having to plan for three months ahead because you could pay to get in on the day; you didn't always have to worry about getting time off work or about getting tickets. But in the 90s that change had begun to take place.'

Selhurst Park

Along with his personable and king-like status, Eric Cantona's character certainly had its fiery side. During the 1993/94 Double season, he was red-carded twice in two consecutive league games, first at Swindon where he stamped on the unfortunate John Moncur, then at Arsenal, after receiving two yellow cards. Earlier that season, he had been sent off on a hostile night at Galatasaray, after which his head had been on the receiving end of a Turkish police baton. Before that there had been controversies in France, including punching a team-mate, calling his coach Henri Michel 'a bag of shit', and throwing the ball at a referee. On one fateful evening in January 1995 at Selhurst Park he was sent off again. The aftermath of the incident would become the most infamous moment of his career and one of the most iconic moments of 1990s football.

That evening, when they visited Crystal Palace, United sat second in the Premier League. In the starting line-up they had their new £7m striker Andy Cole and were well placed to make a strong run for their third title in three years.

It was just after half-time that the chaos came.

Wearing United's all-black change kit, Cantona first kicked out at defender Richard Shaw, then was given his marching orders by the referee, Alan Wilkie. He walked off the pitch towards the dressing room and, as he did so, a Palace fan named Matthew Simmons rushed down the stand to direct some vile abuse his way. 'You fucking cheating French c***,' one witness claimed that Simmons had said. 'Fuck off back to France … French bastard. Wanker.' In response Cantona lashed out, quickly and infamously delivering a flying-kick to the thug before following up with a few punches for good measure. 'Bruce Lee would have been proud of Eric's kung-fu kick,' one team-mate would say of the incident. The shit had truly hit the fan.

'To be honest, we didn't really know what had gone on,' says Walsh, who was at the game that evening. 'I saw Shaw going down and Eric getting sent off, then something happening. But you couldn't really see it. Afterwards, I remember meeting my friend who lived in Croydon and walking back to his house. We put the news on and saw Eric drop-kicking this fella. I thought, "Oh my god." I was just standing there watching the TV because it was repeated over and over again and thinking, "Shit, what's going to happen now?" It just looked like that was the end really.'

United acted firmly, fining Cantona two weeks' wages (£10,800 in total) and banning him from playing until the end of the season. Initially, there had been talk of cancelling his contract. The FA took it further, banning him until the end of September 1995, meaning he would miss the start of the following season. He would also face criminal charges for the incident.

For that court hearing, a bunch of United fans decided to make the journey down to Croydon Magistrates Court. 'We were going there to support Eric and I drove the minibus,' remembers Walsh. 'At the court a load of Palace fans had turned up to give Eric some stick but nobody expected United fans to be there as well. Some of our lot managed to blag themselves inside the courtroom. Eric said later that he was made up to see some friendly faces in there because he had been quite worried about what was going to happen.'

Cantona received a 14-day prison sentence for his actions, which was later reduced to 120 hours of community service coaching football to local youngsters. In the press conference that followed his court case, he would say only this, 'When the seagulls follow the trawler, it's because they think sardines will be thrown into the sea.' Years later, when recalling that night at Selhurst Park, he would say, 'I did not punch him [Simmons] strong enough. I should have punched him harder.'

It would be eight months until Cantona next appeared in a United shirt. Without their talisman his team-mates stuttered, losing in the league away at Everton and Liverpool and drawing at home to Tottenham, Leeds and Chelsea, failing to score in each of those five games. Once again, that season it had been Kenny Dalglish and Alan Shearer's Blackburn Rovers that were United's main challengers, and it was they that took the title on the last day of the season. United would then go on to lose to Everton in a poor FA Cup Final. Their chance of a winning another Double had been blown and Alex Ferguson was not happy. For the following season he would reassess, with big changes to come.

The Return of the King

During the summer of 1995 three big-name players would leave Old Trafford. Paul Ince moved to Italy and Inter Milan for £7.5m. The battling midfielder and his manager had had an increasingly fractious relationship and Ferguson would describe the deal as 'good business'. Andrei Kanchelskis fell out with Ferguson and joined Everton for £5m. Mark Hughes went to Chelsea for £1.5m. Ferguson had wanted to keep his Welsh striker, but with Andy Cole now at the club Hughes saw more opportunities for first-team football away from Old Trafford. There to fill some of the space in the squad was a group of highly rated yet unproven younger players that were emerging from the club's academy.

'The Class of '92', as the group would be known thanks to their success in the FA Youth Cup of that year, included the hard-working defenders Gary and Phil Neville, the diminutive midfielder Paul Scholes and the boy-band-looks wide man David Beckham. Along with Nicky Butt and Ryan Giggs – both similarly youthful but already established in the first team set-up – they would each bring an added vibrancy and dynamism to Ferguson's United, albeit along with significantly less experience.

The youngsters had been nurtured by the club's youth coach Eric Harrison who, according to Gary Neville, 'took boys and turned them into men … made us better footballers and, just as importantly, he made sure we would compete'. Neville would note how he and his fellow graduates possessed 'a relentless will to succeed … an unbelievable work ethic … [and] were desperate to improve … desperate to play for United.'

On the opening day of 1995/96, the new-look and youthful United did not get off to a great start as they lost

3-1 at Aston Villa. Lining up that afternoon had been both Nevilles, Scholes, Butt and Giggs, with Beckham coming off the bench to score. It was a shock result which led to the former Liverpool defender turned pundit Alan Hansen famously remarking on that evening's *Match of the Day*, 'You can't win anything with kids.' The kids recovered well, though, winning each of their next five league games. But nevertheless, after the loss of Ince, Kanchelskis and Hughes, there remained significant work to be done to mount a successful challenge to that season's early pacesetters, Newcastle United. United needed their Cantona.

* * * *

It had been eight months since Selhurst Park, eight months since Cantona had last played in a United shirt. Eight months of him trying to learn the trumpet. But now the King was back.

It was on Sunday, 1 October 1995, at Old Trafford, on Sky Sports against United's great rivals Liverpool.

The fans turned up early. Many wore berets and carried French tricolour flags with Cantona's face on them and the words 'Eric The King'. When he strode out at Old Trafford – last out behind his team-mates, head up, chest puffed out, the collar of his red shirt lifted up – the sense of anticipation and noise were immense.

'The routine for that game was the same as it always was,' remembers Andy Walsh of the day. 'We met up with friends outside the chippy on Chester Road. But there obviously was increased anticipation about him coming back, this returning hero. The atmosphere outside the ground when Liverpool were in town was always good but that day it was a little more special. The anticipation had been building up through all of those months he'd been away.'

That day, the capacity at Old Trafford was restricted to below 35,000 due to the ongoing construction of the new North Stand (officially there were no Liverpool fans in the ground). But inside it was loud and the atmosphere was charged.

In the first two minutes, Cantona set up a goal with a cross to Butt who lifted it past the Liverpool keeper David James for 1-0. The visitors' young striker Robbie Fowler brought them back into it with a fantastic equaliser, then grabbed a brilliant second to put them 2-1 up. But when United earned a penalty on 71 minutes, there was only one man to take it. Back to business and walking up confidently, Cantona struck it calmly past James to equalise. Old Trafford roared and Cantona leaped on to the netting pole behind the goal where he let out a scream of joy at scoring the equaliser on his return.

'Straight away you could see the impact he had on the rest of the players,' says Walsh. 'He had done his puffing out his chest thing, stood there imperiously and you could actually see it in the rest of the players how they were looking up to him. Here was this champion, the leader of the team, and I think you could see the improvement in the way they played now he was back. Even though it was only a 2-2 draw, it was so good. It felt as though we were back together as a club. Everyone was lifted that day and it was the kick the team needed. After that they sort of picked up momentum.'

United next travelled to York City for a League Cup tie. They trailed 3-0 from the first leg (Ferguson had fielded a weakened team at Old Trafford against the Second Division side), but Cantona started at Bootham Crescent and United won 3-1, though they still exited the competition 4-3 on aggregate. An international break followed York, meaning no Premier League fixtures. Instead, United's reserves hosted Leeds's reserves at Old Trafford and Cantona played again – 21,502 turned up, the largest gate in the country that day. There were 30 games of the season left. 'King Eric' was back.

* * * *

By Christmas, Kevin Keegan's Newcastle United led the Premier League table, ahead of United by ten points. It was a significant gap to close, yet for Ferguson's bunch of exciting youngsters and their reliable performers Schmeichel, Irwin, Pallister and Irishman Roy Keane (now in his third season at the club, having emerged as one of United's star men following his move from Brian Clough's Nottingham Forest in 1993), they now had their returning maestro to lift them.

Throughout the run-in, Cantona's impact was simply colossal as he made and scored numerous vital goals for the team, grabbing 13 winners or equalisers himself. From 22 January 1996, United won seven league games 1-0 and he scored the winner in five of them. Out of their last 15 league games, United took 40 points out of 45 as they applied the pressure and closed the gap on Newcastle.

United's comeback was impressive, but the title race that season would be as much about Newcastle's collapse as it would be about the counter from the Old Trafford juggernaut. The Newcastle side that Keegan had built attacked flowingly and won many admirers for their entertaining style of play, but as the season drew on their players became nervous as confidence dipped and points were dropped. By the time the two contenders met at St James' Park on a Monday night in March 1996, the pressure was immense for both sides. Newcastle still had 11 games to go (compared to only ten for Ferguson's men), but their lead over United had been cut to just four points.

That evening St James' was deafening. In the opening exchanges,, striker Les Ferdinand had his chances to put away the game but twice was denied by Schmeichel. Later, Newcastle hit the bar from a free kick. Ferguson's men held on.

On 51 minutes Phil Neville's cross to the far post was met by Cantona who volleyed into the ground and past Pavel Srnicek for what would prove to be the only goal. As he ran off to celebrate, the Frenchman cocked his head back slightly and let out a roar appropriate for such a pivotal moment of the game, and the title race – a visceral release of pent-up passion rooted perhaps in the events of Selhurst and his subsequent banishment.

Andy Walsh hadn't been able to make it up to Newcastle, settling on watching the game on the telly in Manchester. He recalls, 'It was just the logistics of getting there. Working and kick off being on Monday night and what have you. Obviously, I watched it. The performance of the players that day, it made the hairs on the back of your neck stand up.'

With that win – their sixth in a row in the league – United had closed the gap to a single point. As Jim White would note, Cantona's winner 'wasn't just a goal that won a game, it was a goal that assassinated his rivals' hopes'. From then on, Newcastle faltered further as United surged on relentlessly. Through the closing weeks of the season

Ferguson and Keegan would engage in various mind games – or more accurately, Ferguson played mind games with Keegan, the latter famously snapping during one post-match interview. 'I will love it if we beat them. Love it!' he ranted. After Newcastle, Cantona went on to notch winners against Arsenal, Tottenham and Coventry. In the end, United took the Premier League by four points. It was a turnaround totally driven by Cantona, his galvanising impact and goals in those 1-0 games so vital.

There would be one more Cantona winner that season, this time against Liverpool at Wembley in the FA Cup Final.

The contest had brought big expectations from two great rivals: United, Premier League champions; Liverpool, third in the league and with their star striker Robbie Fowler who had scored 36 goals. It was the day when the Liverpool players wore cream Armani suits for their pre-match walk on the pitch. 'We thought they looked like fucking knobs,' the United defender David May would comment of their outfits. The game itself would turn out quite unmemorable with few chances created and entertainment kept to a minimum.

The deadlock was broken on 86 minutes. A corner from Beckham was punched out by David James and the ball fell to Cantona. Having moved back intelligently to the edge of the area, he shaped his body superbly and struck his volley through the Liverpool players and home. In his biography of Cantona, Philippe Auclair would describe the goal as 'a study in poise and elegance'. It won United another Double.

* * * *

The following month, an IRA bomb exploded on Corporation Street in the centre of Manchester. Thanks to a warning call made 90 minutes beforehand, a massive evacuation of the area was made and thankfully no lives were lost, although over 200 people were injured. Earlier in the year, an explosion at Canary Wharf in London had killed two people, ending an IRA ceasefire that was critical to the Northern Ireland peace process.

In the Manchester blast, over 1,000 buildings were damaged, among them the brutalist Arndale Centre. Out of the destruction would come change, as the bomb's devastation cleared the way for the development and rejuvenation of the city centre. In place of the unloved 70s buildings came shiny shops and retail areas, new public spaces and good design: places to visit and live. As the Manchester music man Tony Wilson explained, 'The bomb was a catalyst to the regeneration and gave us a chance to rebuild.'

The King is Dead

In 1996/97, United won the Premier League, again. On the opening day of the season, David Beckham lobbed the Wimbledon keeper Neil Sullivan from the halfway line and that year he and his fellow youngsters from 'The Class of '92' became even more established and influential in the United team. Cantona scored 11 times in the league. Newcastle again had been their rivals, along with Liverpool and Arsenal. Four of the first five Premier League crowns had now gone to Old Trafford and things in the Premier League were getting a bit like *Groundhog Day*, the 1993 Bill Murray movie in which his grumpy weatherman character relives the same day over and over again.

Beyond their dominance in England, that season United made a true push for European glory in the Champions League. They had last won the European Cup in 1968 and in recent years UEFA's three-foreigner rule had hindered them on the European stage – most notably in Barcelona in 1994 as they went down 4-0 in the Camp Nou with Ferguson choosing to play Gary Walsh in goal instead of Peter Schmeichel after being limited by the regulation. With these restrictions now gone, however, an unlimited number of players from European Union countries could be selected in European competition, meaning that United and other clubs had far greater options as to who they could select for their teams.

In 1996/97, having knocked out Porto in the quarter-final, United faced Borussia Dortmund in the last four. Many had fancied United to progress but over two legs they missed a succession of chances and could not break the Germans down, succumbing 1-0 both away and at home and 2-0 on aggregate. Ferguson would describe the Dortmund tie as a 'devastating' exit. '[W]e missed 15 one-v-ones that night,' he would say. The search for that top European prize would continue. Added to that, Eric Cantona was leaving the club.

* * * *

The announcement of the King's retirement from football came on Sunday, 18 May 1997. Cantona had had another strong season with those 11 league goals, plus 12 assists (the most in the Premier League that year). He was still only 30, yet quite suddenly had decided to call it a day. 'I didn't want to play anymore,' he would later say. 'I'd lost the passion.'

'We knew that he had appeared to be getting frustrated with the growing commoditisation of him,' recalls Andy Walsh. ['Manchester,' Cantona would say, 'it's a lot of merchandising. You're sometimes needed for a video, a book, photographs, interviews.'] But I didn't exactly see his retirement coming.

'When it did there was this sense of loss for someone that has been very important to you. Here was someone who you not only had admiration for as a player but who philosophically you felt a kinship with as well. That might seem a bit over-sentimental but that's how it felt as a football fan. It's not just about the football. There just weren't any other players around at the time that were as interesting as him. He was one of the few players you would pay to just go and watch him. Fans that go to Old Trafford now who probably never saw him play will still sing his name. Here was somebody who cared.'

The fans were shocked. The man who had been so influential for their team, who had kicked them on to the title in 1992/93 and contributed so magnificently to their 1995/96 Double while giving them so much joy was leaving. It was the end of an era.

Throughout the 1996/97 season there had been suggestions of how Cantona's bright light had been dimming. Writing in *The Guardian*, David Lacey noted, 'His contribution to the team's fourth championship in five years has been valuable but not invaluable.' Ferguson would later observe how his star man had seemed 'subdued and did not seem to be enjoying his football', adding, 'Somehow the spark had gone.' Nevertheless his manager had tried to persuade him to stay, though his attempts ultimately were in vain.

On the day of the announcement hundreds came to Old Trafford to pay tribute – perhaps for some it was to grieve for the man who had given them so much. It was an abrupt end, leaving like that. But the King – the first real superstar of the Premier League era – was gone.

The dust would eventually settle and Ferguson's United would enter a different phase. Cantona later reflected, 'My best moment? I have a lot of good moments but the one I prefer is when I kicked the hooligan.' Meanwhile for Andy Walsh, the everyman United fan, there would be eventful and changing times ahead.

2

Dancing in the Streets

AWAY FROM the Premier League, on football's international stage, it was the England national team's run to the semi-final of Italia 90 that marked a key staging post in the game's 1990s re-emergence. Attendances after the tournament had risen across the Football League and gradually the game's reputation was built up from that of the 'slum sport' of the previous decade.

For the England team itself, however, the years following Italy turned out to be a disappointment. After the World Cup, Bobby Robson left his post for PSV Eindhoven, having announced his decision to resign before the tournament had started (he had learned that the FA would not be renewing his contract). In his place came Graham Taylor, a man of differing managerial style from his predecessor – he favoured direct play over Robson's more possession-based approach – who through his decade in charge of Watford had brought them up from the Fourth Division to the First and then to Europe.

Taylor's reign as England boss would not be a success. At Euro 92 in Sweden, England drew their first two group games then lost to hosts Sweden to exit before the knockout stages. Taylor's squad selections would often puzzle and draw criticism, such as dropping Paul Gascoigne, leaving out the in-form Chris Waddle and using 59 different players in total (29 of them debutants) during his time in charge. It didn't help either that during this time veterans such as Terry Butcher and Gary Lineker retired from international football. Worse was to come during qualification for the 1994 World Cup when Taylor's England missed out entirely as they failed to reach the finals.

That disastrous campaign was covered in the ill-advised documentary, *An Impossible Job* (also known as *Do I Not Like That*), which followed the England team through that ultimately unsuccessful qualification campaign. Their struggles, and Taylor's demise, were fully captured on camera, along with some of his strange exasperated comments made during extremely pressurised moments:

'What sort of thing is happening here?'

'Can we not knock it?'

And most memorably, 'Do I not like that.'

Throughout his time in charge, Taylor had been relentlessly targeted by the tabloid press. One headline that came after England's defeat to Sweden at Euro 92 read, 'SWEDES 2 TURNIPS 1,' with a picture of a vegetable superimposed on to Taylor's head. In late 1993 he resigned from the job, jumping before he was pushed.

Come the summer of 1994 there would, then, be no place at the finals in America for England and English football fans.

* * * *

FIFA had awarded the 1994 tournament to America in the hope it would open up a nation more interested in American football, baseball and basketball to the world's game. That summer, 24 teams from across the globe converged on the States for the showpiece, month-long event. Matches were to be played played at NFL and college football stadiums in New York, Orlando, Los Angeles, Dallas, Chicago, San Francisco, Detroit, Foxborough (Massachusetts) and Washington. The stadiums were gigantic and while football (soccer) was not America's game, USA 94 would become the best-attended World Cup ever, with crowds averaging 68,991 per game and a total attendance figure of 3.6 million. With the stars of the global game on show, and with supporters from many nations happily mixing together, the tournament would turn out to be a vibrant celebration of football, all in glorious technicolour.

'I was always convinced that, at least from a financial point of view, a World Cup held in the United States was bound to be a colossal success,' wrote the journalist Brian Glanville, veteran of eight World Cups up to that point.

The opening ceremony in Chicago was attended by President Bill Clinton, along with Diana Ross who sang some songs and missed a penalty on the pitch. That same day the former Buffalo Bills NFL star O.J. Simpson was pursued by police in a slow-motion chase along a Californian freeway following his alleged murder of his ex-wife Nicole Brown Simpson (this was America and the action was filmed from helicopters and broadcast live on television). Back in Chicago at the soccer, holders Germany beat Bolivia 1-0 to kick things off.

For USA 94 the journalist Don Watson was given £6,000 to travel around America, following the spectacle of the tournament and writing about what he saw. His book, *Dancing in the Streets: Tales from World Cup City*, captures the full essence of the event and his journey as he takes you with him to the cities he visits and the games he watches on his travels. Watson always seems to be talking to new footballing friends, trying to get a ticket for a game or working out how to get from one city to another. Often he is in a bar. The title of the book comes from the Motown track, 'Dancing in the Street', and when it plays on the jukebox of one New York bar, Watson and some new friends sing along, enthusiastically punching the air as they do.

'I studied a plan of the fixtures and came up with an itinerary,' he explains in the opening pages. 'I would cut a cross section across America, travelling from east to west. I'd start in New York ... then head for places and find out what was going to happen when I got there. Chicago, the city of the Blues ... San Francisco, setting of *Vertigo* ... then the sprawling megalopolis of Weird – Los Angeles and the World Cup Final.'

Best of all in the book is Watson's idea of 'World Cup City' – essentially the places where fans from the competing countries would gather for their games. A kind of mobile city within a city where the fans would stay for the match before packing up and moving on to the next destination.

* * * *

Although England had not made it to America, the Republic of Ireland had. Managed by Jack Charlton, winner of the World Cup with England in 1966, his hard-working and functional team included the likes of Tranmere's John Aldridge, Aston Villa's Paul McGrath and Manchester

United's Roy Keane. They were a strong, committed group and back in Ireland Charlton was a beloved figure. Even in the parochial house on fictional Craggy Island, home to Father Ted Crilly and his dim-witted sidekick Father Dougal McGuire, there was a framed picture of Charlton on the living-room mantelpiece.

New Jersey's Giants Stadium was an hour away from Manhattan and facing Ireland there for their first game was 'Gli Azzuri', The Blues, Italy. 'I had to be there,' insisted Don Watson.

Italy had some of the greatest players in world football playing in what was then the world's greatest league, Serie A. Since 1992, English football fans had been able to follow the league and its stars on Channel 4. There was the Saturday morning magazine show *Gazzetta Football Italia*, presented by the laid-back James Richardson that featured goals from the previous week, subtitled interviews with players and, best of all, Richardson sat in some sunny Italian piazza drinking coffee and translating stories from the Italian football papers. On Sunday afternoons *Football Italia* broadcast live games, attracting over two million viewers. While the Premier League was emerging, it was in Italy at that time that the most glamorous and exotic footballers could be found.

In America, Italy had the goalkeepers Gianluca Pagliuca and Luca Marchegiani. In defence were a young Paolo Maldini, the masterful Franco Baresi, Alesandro Costacurta and Mauro Tassotti. This was the back four of AC Milan, at the time the most formidable in football. The unit had been developed in Milan by the Italy coach Arrigo Sacchi, who between 1987 and 1991 had led the side to a Serie A title and two European Cups. Farther up the field Sacchi's Italy had Dino Baggio, Roberto Donadoni and Antonio Conte, Giuseppe Signori and Pierluigi Casiraghi.

Also they had 'Il Divin Codino', 'The Divine Ponytail' – Roberto Baggio, a forward of such class and ability and character who both created and scored goals for his club Juventus and country. Baggio had a perfect, delicate touch and exuded calmness on the pitch as a number ten operating as a conduit between midfield and attack. World Player of the Year in 1993, a footballing genius and converted Buddhist too. 'If I could try to do the magical, I would,' Baggio once said, 'but always in an effective way. If there's something beautiful about it, it's better. I would do what I felt like doing, what came naturally to me.'

Thousands of Irish fans had made the journey over to New York for the Italy match and, thanks to the city's large Irish and Italian communities, it was the perfect setting for their opening game. The day brought perhaps the high point of Charlton's reign as Ireland manager (arguably even ahead of an excellent run to the quarter-final at Italia 90) as his lads in green beat the Italians 1-0.

The goal came on 11 minutes when Aston Villa's Ray Houghton lobbed the ball over the head of Pagliuca. 'I just thought, "Have a go. See what happens," Houghton said of the moment. When the ball hit the Italian net, the Irish supporters in the stadium went wild. Don Watson was right among the celebrations. 'Everybody is hugging everybody else,' he writes. 'Even a couple of Italians get hugged by mistake … they don't really seem to mind.' It was a superb win for the Irish.

One further memorable moment in New York came when Charlton, dressed in a white, short-sleeved shirt, tie and baseball cap, stood animated and frustrated on the sidelines as despite the heat he was prevented from throwing water bottles out to his players on the pitch.

After New York, Ireland moved on to Orlando where the midday Florida heat would be even more stifling for his players. For the benefit of European television audiences, many of the matches kicked off early throughout the tournament, often to the detriment of teams playing in the hotter host cities. In Orlando, Ireland lost 2-1 to Mexico.

Their tournament would end with a 2-0 defeat to the Netherlands in the second round. Italy, however, would recover and progress. In the second round against Nigeria, Baggio equalised in the last moments of the game before converting the winning penalty in extra time. After Nigeria came Spain; Baggio scored another late winner to send Italy through to the semi-finals.

* * * *

Elsewhere in World Cup City, Brazil had been making their way through the rounds. Brazil hadn't won the World Cup since 1970 – too long a gap for the three-times winners – and at USA 94 they had Barcelona's outstanding Romario and Deportivo La Coruna's Bebeto up front. One of the great sights of the tournament was the whole team, dressed in their bright yellow and green Umbro shirt, walking out in line holding hands. They did it before every game. After advancing unbeaten out of the group stage, they beat the USA 1-0 in the second round in San Francisco. Later, in the quarter-final in Dallas, Bebeto scored twice in a 3-2 win over the Netherlands, including baby-cradling swaying arms celebration for the recent birth of his son.

Heading into the tournament, Brazil's South American neighbours Colombia had been another highly fancied team. Their strong side featured the forward Faustino Asprilla, the crazy-haired midfielder Carlos Valderrama and the charismatic goalkeeper Rene Higuita (who against England at Wembley in 1995 would perform his famous 'scorpion kick' reverse bicycle-kick save). They had been unbeaten in the South American CONMEBOL competition yet in America would deflate. Against the USA, Andres Escobar's own goal led to defeat and two games later they disappointingly exited the tournament at the group stage. After Escobar returned home to Colombia and Medellin his life would end when he was shot dead outside a nightclub following a confrontation with several shady characters. Links between the whole Colombian team and the notorious drug baron Pablo Escobar are explored in the documentary, *The Two Escobars*.

For Argentina's Diego Maradona, World Cup winner in 1986 and now back playing in his homeland with Newell's Old Boys following his time in Europe with Barcelona, Napoli and Sevilla, his World Cup would also end early. A failed drugs test after the Nigeria group game in Foxborough uncovered a cocktail of five banned substances in his body and ended his tournament. Without him, Argentina were beaten 3-2 in their second round tie against Romania. In that game 'The Maradona of the Carpathians', Gheorghe Hagi, had shone. Everything went through him as he set-up one of the goals and scored another.

For Bulgaria meanwhile, their star Hristo Stoichkov had helped steer his country through the tournament. Earlier his goal against Argentina had helped them to a

2-0 group stage win in Dallas, while in their quarter-final against Germany, Stoichkov's sweet free kick levelled the scores against the holders before Yordan Letchkov guided in the winning header for 2-1.

Up to that point USA 94 had been the tournament of heroes, be they failed ones or emerging: Jack Charlton and Baggio; Maradona, Hagi and Stoichkov; even the on-the-run O.J. Simpson.

For Don Watson, World Cup City had become Chicago for Germany against Belgium in the second round. 'By kick-off the wind is icy and a thick layer of cloud has settled over the stadium,' he writes in *Dancing in the Streets*. 'I take my seat a few seats away from a small Belgium division decked out in red wigs.' Germany won 3-2. Next he travelled to San Francisco where he wandered round the city's Chinatown, spent a lot of time in an Irish bar and watched the Sweden-Romania quarter-final in Stanford (the university town an hour away from the city). Sweden won on penalties. Watson's travels continued to be a story of internal flights and more quests for tickets, new stadiums and further conversations with strangers. Add to that some late-night drinking and early-morning writing.

In England, fans watched the terrestrial coverage of the tournament, envious of what might have been had Graham Taylor's side managed to qualify. On the mock news show *The Day Today*, Steve Coogan's TV presenter character Alan Partridge had provided a special guide to the World Cup. An elaborate and interactive presentation of the tournament's complex schedule, his ridiculous contraption provided a plan of the group stage system and overview of the venues and teams on the floor, along with chaotic, moveable signposts above. 'To help us along and add a little bit of colour and fun to the proceedings,' Partridge says, before becoming comically entangled in his 'Soccermeter'.

Watson made his way to the semi-final in Pasadena, a wealthy suburb in Los Angeles's vast sprawl, to watch Brazil-Sweden, Romario and Bebeto. The Brazilians won 1-0 to set up a final with Italy who had beaten Bulgaria on the other side of the country at Giants Stadium. Again, Baggio was the hero with both goals in that game.

On the streets of Pasadena after the Brazil-Sweden semi, Watson joined in the party. 'The place is alive with colour and noise, creating one great joyful throbbing cacophony,' he writes. 'A black sports car with a group of Italians passes a bunch of Brazilians in a green one. "Baggio, Baggio," shout the Italians. "Bebeto! Romario!" Shout the Brazilians.'

* * * *

Like Brazil's semi-final, the 1994 World Cup Final would also be held in Pasadena at its 94,000-capacity open-air Rose Bowl stadium. A few years ago, as some friends and I travelled around LA on a road trip down the California coast, we stopped off (at my request) for a look at the iconic stadium. We parked up and walked round the outside and through an open entrance I could glimpse the stands, plus some of the field where some of the famous moments of the tournament had taken place. That was as close as I got, though, as the security guard wouldn't let me look inside. By this point my friends were getting bored so we left and went to a Target to buy some jeans.

In 1994, Don Watson was still in Pasadena. The tournament and his journey were now approaching their end. At the time the city of Pasadena had a population of around

130,000 and on World Cup Final day it was swamped by soccer fans, creating a carnival of Brazilian yellow and Azzurri blue. '[F]lags are flying from car windows and the whole of Colorado Boulevard is like a honking, bellowing, flag-billowing, bumper-to-bumper jam,' notes Watson, who had spent $400 on his ticket for the game.

As is often the case for such high-profile events, the final was not much of a spectacle: 0-0 all the way, a tussle and a stalemate to the end. 'This is one of those games that never seems to resolve the tension of the first few minutes,' Watson notes, 'the teams taking quick snaps at one another, but never seeming to have the time or the assurance to really build a move.' Extra time came along but the first goalless World Cup Final meant penalties would be required to decide the winner.

Eight kicks had been taken. Five had been scored. Italy had missed two: Baresi and Daniele Massaro. It was 3-2 to Brazil. Then up stepped Roberto Baggio, 'The Divine Ponytail'. His five goals so far in the tournament had taken his country to where they were this moment. Down on the Rose Bowl pitch, the weight of an entire nation's expectations hung on his shoulders.

'When I went up to the spot I was pretty lucid, as much as one can be in that kind of situation,' Baggio would later write in his autobiography.

His run-up was long, beginning in the D on the edge of the area, and step after step he advanced. When he reached the ball, he struck it high – too high – and the ball sailed over the bar.

Baggio, Italy's hero, had missed. All alone, he stood there, hands on hips and head bowed, as the Brazilians celebrated.

'[T]here is no easy explanation for what happened at Pasadena,' he would reflect on his miss. 'Unfortunately, and I don't know how, the ball went up three metres and flew over the crossbar. It was the toughest moment of my career. Before I left for the finals, my Buddhist spiritual master told me that I would be confronted with a lot of problems and that everything would be decided at the very last minute. At the time I didn't realise his prediction would be so accurate.'

In reality, his penalty would have levelled the scores – even if he had put his away, were Brazil to have scored their last kick, they would have won it anyway. But Italy had lost and Brazil had won the World Cup.

'Only those who have the courage to take a penalty miss them. I failed that time … it affected me for years. It's the worst moment of my career. I still dream about it,' Baggio would reflect.

After the game Don Watson walked back into Pasadena, ate a Mexican meal and drank margaritas, raising a toast to the victorious Brazilians. The World Cup was over and World Cup City was over. It was back to real life for everyone. For Watson, it meant heading back to London to finish his story. 'Goodnight, and goodbye, World Cup City.'

3

Our Friends in the North

Sir John

Next stop, True North. Newcastle. The early train was tearing along the East Coast mainline, through York and Durham, on the way to the city on the Tyne. Once it had crossed the bridge, it pulled into the station, then it was out into the freezing north-east morning.

Up the hill and it's not even a ten-minute walk to St James' Park, the giant 52,000-seater Premier League beacon sitting right up there among everything, home since 1892 to Newcastle United FC. On my lap of the ground I pass the statue of one of the club's greatest number nines, Jackie Milburn. 'Wor Jackie', the inscription below the statue reads (around here 'wor' means 'our'). Up and round to the massive Leazes and Milburn stands, then more statues: Bobby Robson, the gentleman of the game and former manager here, and Alan Shearer, the club's other great number nine. Then the famous Gallowgate End.

This is a true football cathedral. A place in the middle of town, a brilliant spot for the fans near to the pubs and not far from the station. 'Football is not a passion on Tyneside, it is a religion,' writes Colin Malam in *The Magnificent*

Obsession. The fans here live and breathe the game and this club. 'I could not live without them,' says one such supporter in Malam's book. 'They are more important than life itself.'

It's nearly 11.30am and I am due to meet Sir John Hall, who was chairman of Newcastle United in the 1990s. The self-made property millionaire invested his money and helped to take Newcastle to places they hadn't been for decades, lifting the club for its army of loyal supporters to almost unimagined emotional heights.

After a short wait downstairs in the Milburn Stand, he steps out of the lift to greet me. At 84 years old, Hall is a welcoming figure dressed in a smart suit – I'd read about his steely eyes. We shake hands and take the lift back up to a hospitality area to talk about his time in charge of this great club and the idea of the Geordie Nation.

'The Geordie Nation is basically the extended area around here,' he begins. 'The region and the people that live here. Basically it's Tyneside and the people's culture and way of life. Going back to the pit villages where I was born, it was all about community. Nobody was ever left alone. If you were a widower, people would come round in the morning to see if you were okay. There was that tremendous sense of social being. The sense of family is still very strong here and belonging is very much a part of that. It's important to us.'

Hall was born in 1933 and grew up north of Newcastle near the mining town of Ashington, the same area where Milburn and the World Cup-winning Charlton brothers Jack and Bobby had grown up. It was in the north-east's coalfields, and at the shipyards that lined the River Tyne and stretched out to the North Sea, that the region's industries and lifeblood lay.

Coalmines had given work and life to villages like Ashington. In the 1980s, over 20,000 people worked in the surrounding pits before they were all but finished off. Today at the Woodhorn Colliery site 20 miles north of Newcastle, the buildings and the pithead-winding wheel are preserved as relics of the past. Inside, its galleries display the works of 'The Pitmen Painters', depicting life working underground, along with the miners' leisure pursuits of racing pigeons, the chippy and football. For over a century, shipyards like Swan Hunter at Wallsend built hundreds of vessels that criss-crossed the waters of the world. What remains of them along the banks of the river sit as remnants of a grander past. 'The shipyards are finished,' wrote Nik Cohn in his late-1990s travelogue of England, *Yes We Have No: Adventures in Other England*. As Sir John explains, 'A change came and once those industries ran out and declined and reached nearly the end of their life there was little left in their place.

'A massive part of life then became about the football. For myself I was brought here by my father when I was eight and it was through the football that I became a member of this Geordie tribe.

'Newcastle has always enjoyed a massive support. It's been tremendous all my life. We've only got one club in this area and I always looked at it in this way: that collectively we have about a million fans in our direct catchment. You can look back at the highs when 68,000 stood on the terraces. Today they get 52,000, but they could comfortably get more if they had a ground big enough.

'On a matchday we'd get the bus into town, the whole family, and get off at the same spot. In the ground I used to stand on a part that was essentially a bank with sleepers holding up the dirt. If you got in there early there was a plank of wood, a shelf, which if you got on it meant you could stand and see the match. If you got in late you had to roll over the heads of the crowd to get to the front and sit down there through the match. Afterwards we caught the bus home. That routine dominated your life.

'So for me and for thousands of others in the region, football was a very important part of our lives. It's a very working-class area and the club's roots are very working-class. That's the Geordie Nation: a working-class area where we are loyal and the working population living their lives through football.'

* * * *

Hall is a miner's son and when he started out in work he spent two decades with the National Coal Board, initially as a mining surveyor. After moving into property development (first residential, then commercial), he made his fortune. In 1986 he opened the sprawling Metrocentre – an American-style shopping mall in Gateshead.

Newcastle had spent much of the 80s in either the Second Division or struggling in the First, selling their best local players one after another – Chris Waddle in 1985, Peter Beardsley in 1987, Paul Gascoigne in 1988. In the early 90s, Hall bought the club for £3m.

'The club basically belonged to the old families and there wasn't any investment going on,' he says. 'It had reached a point where they didn't have the cash to invest and were threatened with relegation to the Third Division. I'd made a lot of money and I was a supporter. It needed someone to put some money in, so I started a takeover. That was 1992. I ended up with about 90 per cent of the shares.

'I remember when I was younger going to the matches and looking up to the old boardroom, not once thinking that one day that I would own it. It was the impossible dream. We never had dreams like that. We were told that we had our place. I was basically like Jack Walker at Blackburn and Dave Whelan at Wigan. We were local millionaires and still fans on the terraces.'

Hall knew that the club first needed stability, then a boost, then progress. Key to that would be changes driven by investment.

'I'm a businessman, so I sat down I asked what did we need do to take this project forward? What did we need to do to make it work? Well, we needed a manager. Ossie [Ardiles] wasn't doing it for us and I was told that Kevin Keegan wanted to come back.'

Keegan had enjoyed a spell at the club between 1982– 84 where the twice European Footballer of the Year had helped steer Newcastle to promotion to the First Division. After leaving the game he had spent time living in Spain and playing golf.

'We did the deal,' says Hall. 'He'd been out of it for a long time, but he still had knowledge of the game, the players and all the rest of it. So we brought him in.'

Keegan's family had been miners and before he was born they had moved to South Yorkshire from the northeast after work had become scarce. After hearing stories from his father, he became aware of his family's origins and understood the Geordie region and the people, their football club and what it meant up here. Recalling when he joined the club as a player, Keegan said, 'It felt like home and, right from the start, there was an incredible sense of belonging, the feeling that I was going back to my roots.'

As manager of Newcastle he would say, 'These people work hard all week, they'll come here on a Saturday and pay their hard-earned money and they want to see you die for the shirt. They like to see you win but more often than not, they want to be entertained.'

Keegan was given Hall's full support and was provided with the finances needed to build the side he wanted. 'Yes, we backed him,' says Hall. 'It was just like in a business: you back your managers. You need somebody to run the business so you back them and we backed him fully.'

Crucially, thanks to Keegan's profile in the game, he was able to attract top players to the north-east. 'The players definitely came for Keegan. For me, that was always the interesting thing. You know, trying to get the better players to move this far north was always very difficult. But when you had the right manager the players came for him.'

Early Keegan signings included the defenders Barry Venison from Liverpool and John Beresford from Portsmouth, and the midfielders Paul Bracewell (Sunderland), Rob Lee (Charlton) and Scott Sellars (Leeds United). 'They were his players,' says Hall, 'his choice of player for his choice of football and he basically let them be as creative as they wanted to be. The results were wonderful.'

Under Keegan, in 1991/92 Newcastle managed to retain their status in the Second Division, assuring safety on the last day of the season at Leicester City. The following year they won promotion, romping home in style with 96 points.

In 1993/94, they came third in the Premier League with striker Andy Cole, a £1.75m signing from Bristol City the previous season, scoring 41 times in all competitions. Swarming and creating all around him in the black and white Newcastle shirts were Beresford, Sellars and Lee, along with the Wallsend Boys Club lads Steve Watson, Lee Clark and Peter Beardsley (the latter having been brought back to the club from Everton). Crosses were flying in from out wide, full-backs were pushing on and a vibrant drive was coming from midfield. 'Go out and do what you're good at,' was Keegan's approach. '[P]lay football, pass the ball quickly, find space, put the ball in the net.' Keegan's team would be labelled the 'Entertainers'.

'I couldn't wait to see another game,' says Hall. 'You just couldn't wait. It was unbelievable football. It just flowed. That's what everybody loved about it.'

The fans were having a great time and there was a palpable excitement in the city. Paul Ferris, a former player with the club who by now was part of Keegan's medical staff, would describe Newcastle at the time as being 'an incredible place to be … a warm and friendly club … His [Keegan's] charisma and philosophy rubbed off on all those who came into contact with him.'

Off the pitch, great progress was also being made as St James' Park was rebuilt. Between 1992 and 1996, £20m was spent on the construction of new stands that would transform the ground from crumbling concrete with open-air toilets into a polished 36,000-capacity Premier League stadium. The club had 34,000 season ticket holders and demand for tickets could not be satisfied. Further development of the Leazes and Milburn stands would be completed by 2000, creating a huge white-painted cantilever roof that could be seen from across the city and which would increase capacity to 52,000.

In 1994/95, the trajectory of Newcastle's progress stuttered slightly with a sixth-place finish in the Premier League, yet hopes for the future remained high. When

Cole was controversially sold to rivals Manchester United in 1995 for £7m with winger Keith Gillespie arriving at St James' as part of the deal, the fans were not happy. Keegan, though, weathered the storm and asked to be trusted. 'I felt we could take it [the deal] on and you've got to allow me to do that,' he told a group of disgruntled fans gathered outside the ground after Cole was sold. 'If it doesn't work, I know what the implications are. I know what the bottom line is.'

Keegan would continue to build. The club was going places.

Sir Les

In the summer of 1995, Keegan was given more than £14m to sign four new players who it was hoped would help propel his side to the next, championship-winning level. Goalkeeper Shaka Hislop arrived from Reading for £1.6m. Defender Warren Barton cost £4m from Wimbledon. The skilful French international winger and future shampoo-advert star David Ginola joined from Paris Saint-Germain for £2.5m. And brought in to fill the boots of Cole and be the figurehead goal-scorer of the 'Entertainers' was the pacy and powerful England international Les Ferdinand, arriving from Queens Park Rangers for £6m.

Three hundred miles away from Newcastle, in west London, is Loftus Road, home of Queens Park Rangers Football Club. Les Ferdinand – or 'Sir Les' as he had been known in his playing days – is director of football here. More than a decade on from the end of a playing career that brought near to 200 goals for a host of clubs, he is sat in an executive box overlooking the Loftus Road pitch, remembering his move north to Newcastle in 1995.

'In terms of a team and the way they played I knew who I was moving to,' he recalls. 'I admired the way they played and I knew about the manager. I hadn't worked for him, but I had been so impressed with what he'd done with Newcastle up to that point. He had wanted to sit down with me before I joined to talk about the team and what he wanted from me and I knew I wanted to be a part of what was happening up there.

'I was bought to score goals and I think the previous season I'd got something like 26 for QPR, so I felt that going into Newcastle was about keeping that momentum going. Being part of that team was a centre-forward's dream. There was Ginola on one side sending in crosses, Gillespie on the other; Peter Beardsley was just behind me, Rob Lee just behind him. I used to ask them just to put the ball into the area and I would go and attack it. They never let me down with that, to be honest. I felt like there would always be goals.'

The 'Entertainers' started 1995/96 in explosive form as they won nine of their first ten league games in an exciting, swashbuckling, attacking style. Early in that run Ginola notched a fine edge-of-the-area strike as they won 2-0 at Sheffield Wednesday. Ferdinand, meanwhile, raced to 13 goals. His range included fast runs finished with powerful strikes or precise headers. He was the complete centre-forward, a magnet for the ball and devastating in front of goal. 'You want to get off to a great start and we did,' says Ferdinand. 'We were winning and I was scoring. It was great.'

As the results and momentum built up for Newcastle, so too did the mood and belief around the club. 'It was probably the best atmosphere you could wish for as a footballer. We were playing a brand of football that everyone was enjoying. The ground was sold out and the atmosphere on matchdays was very special. With each win it, built and built and the whole place was bouncing. In fact the whole city was bouncing, really riding the crest of something good that was happening. Everyone was so engrossed with all of the players and there wasn't a day where I didn't come out of my house and I'd sign an autograph. Everyone knew where you lived but that was fine. There was a real nice feeling about the place.'

Training sessions were held at the club's Durham University base and thousands of fans would turn up – it was open and inclusive as Keegan fostered a connection between the players, the idols and the supporters. They even had burger vans for the crowds just like for matchdays at St James' Park. Everybody was welcome and the region was totally behind the team.

Even the future leader of the country, Tony Blair, got involved. As MP for Sedgefield since the 1980s, Blair and his on-the-rise New Labour party had moved to align itself with things that people actually liked. He did things like turning up to music awards shows to mingle with the stars and, being a Newcastle fan, doing headers in a photo opportunity with Keegan. 'He wasn't that bad with a ball,' Blair's spin-doctor Alistair Campbell would say.

The Newcastle kits were special that year too, made by Adidas with grandad collars (a nod to the early 1900s when the club won three league titles in five seasons). The Newcastle Brown Ale logo, with its five-point-star city skyline silhouette, was plastered on them. Apparently, over 500,000 Newcastle shirts were sold that season and on a matchday St James' was a sea of black-and-white-shirted fans. 'The Tyne Bridge was on the front of the Newcastle strip,' Martin Hardy would write in *Touching Distance*, his look-back book of that season. 'It was a shirt worn with pride ... The team looked ready for business.'

As a youngster I think I had that kit and I can remember watching that exciting Newcastle side on the TV that season. Also at that time was the BBC series *Byker Grove*, which formed part of the key *Newsround-Byker-Neighbours* after-school trilogy. Back then, all things Geordie seemed all right to me.

* * * *

By late January 1996, Newcastle were 12 points clear of Manchester United in the Premier League title race. Following defeat at Old Trafford just after Christmas their lead had been cut to ten points, but afterwards they had recovered again to win their next five games. In February Keegan further bolstered his side's attacking options by adding the Colombian maverick Faustino Asprilla for £7m from Italian side Parma. How could Newcastle be stopped now? Even with several months of the season left to go, many considered the 1995/96 Premier League crown to be on its way to the north-east.

'Peter Beardsley had done the calculations,' says Ferdinand. 'If we'd have continued in the vein we were in we would have had the league wrapped up by the last few weeks in March, or something like that. I think at that point some of the players thought it was ours for the taking. We had the big lead.

'When we lost the first game, there wasn't necessarily the sense of thinking, "Damn, we've lost three points here, we've better not lose any more." It was a little more complacent than that: "We've lost three points but we're still quite a way clear."

'Looking around the changing room, there weren't that many of us who had actually won anything major. A fair few of us in there probably didn't know what it was like to take a team across the line in that situation. Also we had some of the players who were key for us in the early part of the season having a spell of not performing in the way they'd been performing before. I include myself in that category. That's always going to happen through a season, people are going to have off-patches, but too many players had off-patches at the same time. At the same time Man United were beginning to close the gap and piling on the pressure.'

Gradually Newcastle's form began to dip and the wheels began to fall off their title challenge. A 2-0 defeat at West Ham then a 3-3 draw at Manchester City meant valuable ground was given up to Manchester United who won twice over the same spell. Five points were given up over two games.

The statistics show that in the last 14 matches of the season Newcastle's wins dried up as only 18 points were picked up compared to Manchester United's Eric Cantona-inspired 37. In the end Alex Ferguson's men would kill the dream on Tyneside, reversing the lead that had previously appeared insurmountable and grabbing the league for themselves. For Newcastle, it was a capitulation capitalised on by an unstoppable juggernaut.

The turning point in the race came in March 1996 as Newcastle hosted Man United at St James'. That day – a Monday thanks to Sky TV scheduling – 'Tyneside came to a standstill,' wrote Martin Hardy in *Touching Distance*. 'The air around St James' Park was electric [with] fear and hope.' The visitors' Steve Bruce, another Wallsend Boys Club product and future Newcastle manager, would recall how in the ground, 'It was a phenomenal atmosphere, it was absolutely crackling ... 36,000? It sounded like 96,000.'

As the game got under way under the floodlights, it was Newcastle that started the strongest with Ferdinand twice testing Peter Schmeichel. 'I remember breaking through on a couple of occasions and having a couple of good efforts,' says Ferdinand, 'but Schmeichel saved both of them. For the second one I thought I'd slotted it past him. We hit the crossbar as well. We'd hit all sorts but we just couldn't score. Looking back, it was difficult to play better than we did in the first 45 minutes of that game. Then in the second half they stepped it up and got the result. Cantona, 1-0. They didn't have many chances, but, bang, it was in the back of the net and that was it.'

The vital win had been snatched away. Tyneside was stunned and the defeat proved a seismic blow to Newcastle's challenge. Their lead was cut to a single point.

Later that month they were finally overtaken. Then came Liverpool away, a 4-3 defeat at Anfield, one of the most famous games of the Premier League era – a true classic which saw Newcastle surrender a 3-2 lead and lose it in injury time after Stan Collymore's strike. That night had demonstrated the full glory of Newcastle's swashbuckling attack along with their inability to close down and finish off a game. The defeat virtually condemned the Geordies to second place.

'That game was a classic,' says Ferdinand, who scored an equaliser that night. 'But it was another massive blow to our season. I remember in the second half someone going down injured and the physio coming on to treat them. I went and picked up a bottle and as I was drinking remember sort of looking round and thinking that everyone who's watching this today is watching one hell a game. It was probably 3-3 at the time, whatever it was, and the place, a great football stadium, was just fantastic. Both teams were playing some outstanding football and despite what it actually meant for us, I still thought, I'm glad I'm a part of this.

'I remember coming off the pitch at the end of the game and going into the changing rooms. Usually after a loss everyone is kind of quiet. That night no one could actually believe we had lost. Liverpool had played some good football. So had we. Everyone was at a loss for what to say. The manager just said something like, "How could I hammer anyone today? This is one of the best games of football I've ever seen in my life. We've lost but how can I have a go because that's the kind of football I wanna watch."

'That match was definitely another momentum shifter in our season. I actually think that if we would have won that game we would have gone on to win the league. You have moments in the season that give you a boost. Something that gives everyone a little more self-belief. I think that if we won that game, held on at 3-2 maybe, then it would have given us the belief to go on and win the title.'

There were still seven matches left to play, but for Newcastle the dream looked to be fading. Things were getting to Keegan, too. After beating Leeds United away with two games of the season left to go, there would be his infamous headphones-on-and-finger-pointing 'I will love it' rant on TV. Reacting to Alex Ferguson's 'mind games' needling, the pressure on Keegan had built and built and the emotion came out.

Some would mock Keegan for his passionate outburst, but not Ferdinand. 'The one thing that all supporters want to see from their players is them wearing their hearts on their sleeves,' he says. 'If a player does it, it's strength. But if a manager does it, the perception is that it's a sign of weakness. So for me what he did after Leeds wasn't weak, it was passionate. I remember thinking then, and still when I see it now, "Wow, good on ya, boss.". I didn't think any worse of him for it. Ferguson knew how to rile people up but Keegan cared. I don't think it affected the players in any way.'

* * * *

When it was all over, the Premier League trophy went to Manchester, again. In his programme notes for the last game of the season, Keegan wrote, 'The season lasts 38 matches and the team that finishes top will finish there strictly on merit.' Newcastle drew with Tottenham that day. Manchester United won at Middlesbrough and took the title by four points.

For Ferdinand, the club's top scorer that season with 29 strikes, it was a disappointing end to what otherwise had been a positive season. 'There had been so many highs that year but without a shadow of a doubt not managing to win it was the most disappointing moment of my career. Being so close but in the end falling short,' he said.

Back in Newcastle and sat upstairs at St James' Park, Sir John Hall recalls how disappointing the end to that season had been. 'When we were 12 points clear we were actually planning the victory parade,' he says. 'But it went wrong and it is one of the most disappointing moments of my life. If we had won the league then we would have had a greater confidence in ourselves. We would have progressed after that. We had been losing games and it had gone wrong. It was unfortunate, but it just went wrong.'

After the Tottenham game on the last day of the season there was still a big party in Newcastle. Despite the disappointment of losing their golden chance at glory, the fans still had a good time. This was Newcastle and the Geordie Nation and throughout the Kevin Keegan days there would be hope and optimism all around. Maybe for the 'Entertainers' things could only get better?

The Back Page

After my meeting with Sir John at St James' I step outside and make my way down to St Andrew's Street and The Back Page, a sport books and football memorabilia shop. Outside this gem of a place a black-and-white flag for NUFC hangs outside, while inside the shelves are lined with hundreds of different football titles (even my own effort on Sheffield Wednesday, *Owls*, is there). It has Newcastle match programmes, t-shirts, postcards, DVDs, stickers and mugs (I buy one that says 'Ho'way the Lads'). I meet the shop's owner, a passionate Newcastle fan named Mick Edmondson.

For many years Edmondson has loyally followed Newcastle across the land. He hasn't missed a home game since 1977. In the 90s, he wrote a fanzine, *Toon Army News*, and in 2003 he opened this shop. There is another branch out in Gateshead at Sir John Hall's Metrocentre.

'In the 90s there was the Sportspages which I used to go to when I went to London for Newcastle away games,' he explains in his warm Geordie accent. 'I'd go there to look around and sell the fanzine. I was a big fan of *Viz* magazine, so mine was a bit like that, a football *Viz*. Not so much the cartoons but with, like, a problems page, a crap jokes page and reports from the away matches. I used to go in and see them in the shop and just loved it, so I opened one in Newcastle which was half football half music. That was the first one.

'I always wanted one in the city centre and I used to look at some of the stuff that the club shop sold which apart from the shirts was usually tat. I thought I could do better so I opened up here.'

Edmondson was there through the 90s, the Keegan-Hall era, and went even further back, to Keegan's first spell with the club as a player.

'With Keegan it was just brilliant, you know. A European Player of the Year playing for us in the Second Division. We'd be travelling with thousands of fans all over the country, thousands of us going everywhere to see him and the lads. There'd be 70 coaches lined up down near the train station for an away day. They were two great years when he was playing here. Obviously we got promoted and we had five seasons in the First Division. We started off okay but got rid of Waddle and Beardsley. Gazza had come through but he left too. Then it was back to the Second Division for us.

'At the beginning of the 90s, we lost the play-off semi-final to Sunderland of all people. There was a big pitch invasion – hundreds of Newcastle fans on the pitch. There were police dogs and everything. They reckon they had spare goal posts ready to go in case they got damaged and the match got cancelled. A spare goal so they could finish the match! Anyway, Sunderland went to Wembley and got beaten by Swindon. But Swindon got found out for financial irregularities, so were kicked out of the Premier League and Sunderland got promoted. They'd finished sixth and we'd finished third, but they got promoted. You couldn't make it up. So the 90s got off on a bit of a downer to be honest.

'Then John Hall came in and took over. He had the vision. He'd built the Metrocentre and brought Keegan back to the club. That was great. We'd had Ossie [Ardiles] but we needed a leader. We needed Keegan. He saved us. The last game of the season away at Leicester, we needed a win to stay up. We were 1-0 up, but they scored right at the end to make it one each. Then we went straight up to the other end and they let in an own goal. We won and stayed up. The other result actually went our way anyway, so we didn't have to win. I think we stayed up by four points in the end.

'Keegan bought some great players in after that, Rob Lee, John Beresford, Barry Venison, and we won the first 11 games the next season. Thirty-three points out of 33. Then he signed Andy Cole. We had started buying and we went up.'

Despite the heartbreak of Newcastle's collapse a few years later, 1995/96 is one season that Edmondson fondly remembers.

'That year was great,' he says. 'It was unbelievable what Keegan had built up. As fans we couldn't believe what was happening. The ground was built up and had taken shape and the atmosphere was amazing. Sky TV had just happened. We had the best strip, the kit, and the team was great and so exciting to watch. We were everyone's second team. It was like a dream. Everything was coming right. Everyone thought we were going places. It was a great time in a great town. Great, great happy days.

'Even when Keegan lost his cool on the telly, 99 per cent of people in Newcastle loved it because they thought, "He's got passion. He's one of us." We weren't laughing at him, we were thinking, "Come on, Keegan!"

'After the Tottenham game [the last of 1995/96] it was crazy. The fans were jumping off roofs, jumping off window ledges on to lampposts and everything. It was like we'd won the league. It was mental. The whole city was partying. You thought it was going to be like that forever.'

* * * *

In the summer of 1996, Keegan and Hall's Newcastle made their next big move – a huge statement of intent – as they broke the world transfer fee record to sign Blackburn Rovers' star striker Alan Shearer for £15m. The previous record had been Gianluigi Lentini's £13m move from Torino to AC Milan in 1992 and the next highest fee paid in England had been Stan Collymore's £8.5m transfer from Nottingham Forest to Liverpool three years later.

At Blackburn, Shearer had finished the Premier League's top scorer in each of the previous four seasons, including in 1994/95 when they won the title. Strong and totally devastating in front of goal, Shearer had just scored five times for England during that summer's European Championship and was definitely the most coveted talent in the country.

Shearer was also a Newcastle lad, the son of a sheet metal worker who had grown up in the city and stood on the terraces at St James' Park. He loved Newcastle, but as a youngster had slipped through the net and moved to Southampton. Ten years later at the age of 26, the boy turned man was coming home. He would be paid an estimated £30,000 a week to do so.

The press conference for his record transfer took place inside the ground on the eve of the new season. Some 1,500 workers from the brewery across the road were given the afternoon off from making Newcastle Brown Ale, so they could be there. Sat at the table, Shearer was flanked by his new manager and Hall.

'I've always said I've wanted to play for Newcastle at some stage,' Shearer said, 'and I want to play for Newcastle with the best years in front of me.'

'It's a great day – a great day for the club,' said Hall. '[W]e have found the right player in Alan. He's a Geordie and I feel a great sense of pride in bringing him back to the north-east.'

'[T]he number nine shirt, St James' Park, the Gallowgate, Newcastle United has always been the dream,' Shearer said.

Afterwards Shearer put on his black-and-white-striped Newcastle shirt, complete with his name and the number nine on his back, and was unveiled to the crowd outside.

Thousands had turned up to witness his return. With arms aloft and spread wide – a pose that preceded by a few years Antony Gormley's 'Angel of the North' sculpture which stands tall near the A1 on the approach to Newcastle – Shearer stood there proudly before the gathered Toon Army.

'I was there in the car park that day,' remembers Edmondson. 'About 10,000 people were there or something like that. It was amazing. We'd bought him. He was going to take us on to the next level. His goals were going to win us the championship. The whole thing was great. I couldn't believe it.'

Newcastle got 1996/97 off to a good start with Ferdinand and his new strike partner Shearer knocking in the goals – 12 between them as they won seven of their first nine games. By October they were top of the league.

That month Manchester United visited St James'. In contrast to the intensity and impact of the 1-0 defeat they had suffered the previous March, when the momentum of the title race had swung in the visitors' favour, this time they were blown away by a 5-0 margin. Shearer and Ferdinand were both on the scoresheet, as was Philippe Albert who chipped the stranded Peter Schmeichel from well outside of the area. It was a perfect performance.

* * * *

After those positive beginnings to the season, however, things began to unravel for Keegan's men. Plans progressed to take Newcastle United into public ownership on the stock exchange (just as Tottenham Hotspur had in the late 80s and Manchester United had in 1991). This would spark a series of events that would ultimately lead to the departure of the club's inspirational manager and, in turn, the team's eventual drop from the top echelons of the Premier League.

Earlier in the day Sir John Hall had explained to me how the business side of the club had become ever more important during his time at the helm. 'When we first came in it was all about the sport, the football,' he said. 'To the fans it was all about football. But we were businessmen, so to us it was about football and business, about getting money for the football team to do well. You've got to get the cash to put it into the football, the team, so everything you develop at the club to achieve that goal has to be around that. We started developing everything. The entertainment side was bringing in a good amount to the club, the corporate side as well, the merchandising, the shirts and everything like that. That was very important. It was about marketing the club.' Between 1993/94 and 1996/97, the club's turnover increased from £17m to £40m.

Newcastle would go on to raise over £47m in the public flotation, with the club then valued at over £180m. Much of the cash was used to pay off existing debt built up over the previous few years – predominantly for the development of the stadium, plus some to cover instalments on transfer fees for players that had already been signed. The result of this process? The club was now answerable to its investors.

For Keegan the upcoming flotation and the changes happening on the business side of things at the club did not sit well with him. '[It] was changing all our lives,' Keegan would later say. 'To my mind it was not the way to run Newcastle United … this was no longer the club I knew and loved. It was becoming a totally different organisation: suddenly the flotation had taken over everything … I could feel the control slipping away.'

Along with these commercial challenges Keegan had also realised that the drama of the previous season had taken quite a toll on him, particularly emotionally. '[I]t took an awful lot out of me,' he would say. 'I was absolutely drained.' He had strongly considered leaving at that point and speaking in later times he would admit that he 'wasn't enjoying my job.

I had to be honest with myself, I wasn't even enjoying going in to training every day … I was feeling jaded.'

With the club about to become a plc, however, a commitment was needed from him to stay on as manager and sign a new two-year contract. 'You either sign it or you go,' Keegan was told. It is said that he offered to stay until the end of the season, but due to the turbulence that such a scenario would have caused for the flotation and share price, he would have to go. 'I didn't jump, I was pushed,' Keegan would say.

It was a sad end to Keegan's five years with the club – a mid-season split from the team he had built and the fans that worshipped him. But this was the 1990s when off-field financial factors were becoming ever more influential.

For Mick Edmondson, stood in his shop, The Back Page, it was a huge blow. 'I thought we were going for the title again. We were going to win the league that year. We had Shearer on top of what we had the season before. We *were* going to win it. But Keegan left and it didn't quite work out like that.'

As one supporter would say on a radio phone-in after the news had broken, 'People are saying that Kevin leaving is like the Queen dying, but it's worse than that.'

In Keegan's place came the legendary former Liverpool player and manager Kenny Dalglish, last seen guiding Blackburn – and Shearer – to the 1994/95 Premier League title. Under him, Newcastle would secure a second-placed finish behind Manchester United as Shearer and Ferdinand finished the season with 41 top-flight goals between them.

Newcastle could have kicked on after that and challenged again. But they didn't. Ferdinand left for Tottenham along with David Ginola and Shearer's

1997/98 season was hit by injury. Players of lesser quality were brought in – Des Hamilton, Jon Dahl Tomasson, Alessandro Pistone, Andreas Andersson – and that year they finished 13th in the table. They would finish in the bottom half of the Premier League in each of the three seasons that followed.

Looking back at 1995/96, that had been the moment for Newcastle. They could have done it. But they didn't take their chance and it passed them by.

* * * *

The flotation took place in late 1997 and not long afterwards Sir John Hall stepped down as chairman. 'I've done everything I've set out to achieve,' he said. 'I don't think any other club in England has made the progress we have in the last five years.'

In March 1998 there came the embarrassing episode of the club's new chairman Freddie Shepherd and his deputy Douglas Hall (Sir John's son) caught mocking the club's fans, its players and the women of Tyneside during a 'Fake Sheikh' *News of the World* sting. In a Spanish hotel and then in a lap-dancing club, recordings caught the pair referring to the supporters as 'mugs' for buying replica shirts and other merchandise, labelling Alan Shearer as 'boring' and explaining how they thought 'Newcastle girls are dogs'. It was a pretty sorry episode for the Premier League club.

'Obviously it was a total set-up,' says Edmondson. 'Some blokes do say things when they've had a drink or think they are in private company or whatever. I'm sure they regretted it. But it was embarrassing. They live a life where they've got all the money in the world and if they want to spend it on this or that, then that's their choice. It was disappointing to hear it at the time and it was a very negative thing to come out for our club. Our supporters didn't deserve that and, you know, the women round here definitely didn't deserve that!' Shepherd and Douglas Hall would step down from their positions, though both would subsequently return to their posts.

Under Dalglish, Newcastle lost the FA Cup Final in 1998 and again in 1999 under his successor, Ruud Gullit. It approaches a century since the club last won the top league in English football.

As I leave The Back Page, Edmondson explains what it will be like at the match tomorrow and what all of this, Newcastle United, means to him. 'There'll be 52,000 people there,' he says. 'You'll see it. The pubs will be packed. Everyone will be having a good time. It's like a drug. We go every week. You just go because you love it. It's unconditional love. *Unconditional Love* – that's what I'd call my autobiography. It's what you do on a Saturday afternoon or Sunday, or next Wednesday. It's what you do and I love it.'

* * * *

After my journey up this morning and my chats with Sir John Hall and Mick Edmondson I feel like a pint.

It's fair to say that 1927 was a great year up here. It was the year United last won the First Division title and it was the same year Newcastle Brown Ale was created. Sat in the shadow of St James' is The Strawberry, a proper football pub that gets really busy on matchdays and which has framed photos on the walls of NUFC's past: Shearer,

Keegan, Ferdinand (signed), Bobby Robson, Chris Waddle and many more. I settle down for a drink of the 'Broon'.

Across the way is where the brewery once stood, where on the day of Alan Shearer's unveiling its workers had filed over to the ground to welcome home their returning son. The brewery's gone now and according to the bottle I have Brown Ale is made in Tadcaster, North Yorkshire. Today, standing on the old brewery site is a hotel with a plaque on the wall, a Brown Ale five-point star, lit up there in a bright blue nod to the past.

Geordie Nation

The morning after the night before. Today is matchday and I walk down to the Quayside for a coffee and a read. The local press are covering the big issues. In *The Chronicle*, it's Newcastle's 125th anniversary. The lady who sold it me called me 'pet'. In *Viz*, 'The Real Ale Twats' are spreading their good word, 'Let us take our places at the bar and converse with strangers about the virtues of cask-conditioned ale.' The river runs by.

I wander across the sweeping Millennium Bridge to Sir Norman Foster's shiny and curvy Sage arts venue. From this side of the river – technically I'm in Gateshead – you face back into Newcastle and across the water are two of its great sights. To the left, the arching green Tyne Bridge, which dominates and dwarves the buildings below. In the 1998 TV series *Our Friends in the North*, which followed a group of friends and their intertwining up-and-down lives from the 1960s to the 90s, the epic crossing formed a prominent and iconic backdrop to some of its scenes. Beyond that and up the hill, peeping through the buildings, is the outline of St James' huge cantilever stands. Later on today, 52,000 will make their way up there. Television has the game tonight, so a 3pm kick-off against Leicester City has become 5.30pm.

In town I see the black-and-white scarves of fans walking around. Replica shirts peek out from jackets. The Geordie Nation is gathering. Closer to kick off The Strawberry is as rammed as expected, so I drop down the hill to the quieter Newcastle Labour Club. Brown Ale and Newcastle shirts are everywhere and, like The Strawberry last night, there are pictures on the wall of past players and legendary moments. Notable from the 90s are Shearer and Ferdinand and the 1995/96 team celebrating a goal. Keegan is up there, as is a young Gazza. In the club there are a fair few blokes wearing the original Adidas 1995/96 shirts, the black-and-white home and marroon-and-blue away ones. All are kept in good condition and reeled out just for matchdays, I imagine.

Along with it being the club's 125th birthday, talk around town has been of a possible overseas takeover. Billionaire owner Mike Ashley, the boss of retailer Sports Direct, bought the club back in 2007 for over £130m and since then Newcastle have been relegated from the Premier League twice, returned immediately on both occasions but only once have they finished higher than tenth position in the table.

Ashley, an outsider, is not a popular figure up here. 'Few, it seems, are better at stirring up apathy on Tyneside than him,' Duncan Hamilton wrote in *Going to the Match*, his account of a year of watching football matches. 'Ashley looks in profile like a plump Roman emperor,' Hamilton continues. 'The image hardens whenever, from his lofty seat in the stands, he folds his arms and looks hopelessly exasperated or rather bored, his expression blank and staring.'

Previous moves by Ashley to install individuals such as Chelsea's 1990s Rottweiler captain Dennis Wise into senior positions at the club, or renaming St James' Park the Sports Direct Arena, and turning the club shop into a branch of that chain, have not endeared him to the faithful. There have been complaints over the level of investment in the playing side. Allowing a payday loans company to plaster its logo on the famous Newcastle shirt also appeared questionable.

When Keegan returned for a second spell as manager in 2008, he lasted less than a year, citing troubles working under the Ashley regime as well as a lack of control and interference from above with player transfers. 'It's my opinion that a manager must have the right to manage and that clubs should not impose upon any manager [things] that he does not want,' Keegan would later say. A £2m pay-off for constructive dismissal eventually followed.

There have been fan protests demanding Ashley's removal, chants and vitriol from the club's loyal supporters. Ashley didn't seem to care and continued to display an alleged 'wilful neglect from a man that simply doesn't even pretend to care about the club or its supporters', as one article in a later edition of the fanzine *True Faith* would write. The banners seemed to agree, 'He is only one man, we are a city', proclaimed one. A feeling of disenfranchisement lingers among many of the club's fans and thoughts of challenging the elite Premier League clubs from Manchester, London or Merseyside seem a distant dream. Talks of takeovers that have not gone anywhere have further frustrated. As I write, the billionaire remains.

* * * *

Inside St James', there are raking stands that reach up to the huge skylight cantilever roof of the Millburn and Leazes stands. The atmosphere is building. The saxophone song 'Local Hero', composed by Blyth man Mark Knopfler, plays out loud. Banners are held up and flags are waved.

Rafa Benitez won the European Cup for Liverpool but has a big job on here as Newcastle's manager. Financially his hands are very much tied, but he does his best and the fans like him. With his cuddly paunch, glasses and goatee, he conducts the play as his Newcastle side find their way following their return to the top division. They play fairly well and take the lead, get pegged back, go behind then recover to 2-2. Ultimately, an own goal with four minutes left gives Leicester the win.

It's a point dropped and the ground empties straight into town, with the bars and the pubs quickly filling up. People around me seem to be taking the defeat fairly well and don't look too downcast'. They are here with their friends and family, it's Saturday night and for Newcastle this is their first season back after promotion to the Premier League. They'll finish tenth by its end.

Walking down to the station for my train home I think of what Mick Edmondson said to me about that day in 1996 when Manchester United won the Premier League and his beloved Newcastle did not. When people were jumping off roofs and window ledges, boozing and partying into the night. What, I wonder, would it have been like up here if they had actually won it?

4

A Stadium for the 90s

Building of the Year

I head down to London and take the tube to Putney Bridge, before walking over the river to find the offices of Populous, the sports architects who have designed the new Wembley stadium (with Foster & Partners), Tottenham's new £1bn home, and back in 1994 when they were known as The Lobb Partnership, the new stadium for Huddersfield Town.

The banner that hangs outside their building reads 'Drawing people together'. Inside, there are photos of past projects and intricate scale models – the Aviva Stadium in Dublin, the London Stadium for the 2012 Olympics, Sochi's 2014 Winter Olympics stadium.

I meet with Dale Jennins who was site architect at Huddersfield and who has prepared for our chat by digging out the original drawings of the stadium. He has them neatly placed on the table in front of us, while photos of the ground at various stages of construction are projected on to a big screen.

'I was at university in Liverpool and was a Liverpool season ticket holder,' Jennins begins. 'I suppose that being a football fan in the 1980s you were brought up half-expecting to be treated badly when you were around football grounds. Many were completely dilapidated and I suppose you could foresee some of the issues that came out of that.

'After the Hillsborough disaster I think the only decision going forward was that the standing areas had to go. These days you can talk about the different ways that something like that could be approached – safer standing areas as one example – but in those days, and especially for me as a Liverpool fan who was actually there and seeing what I did, we all accepted that all-seater would then be the way forward. I was already a bit interested in stadiums anyway and being an architecture student the thinking and vision for me was that something like Hillsborough would never happen again.

'At university I had to go to do a year out in industry, so I just applied to companies that were doing stadium work. That's pretty much how I ended up being where I am now.

'In my last year at university I designed a stadium for my final dissertation project and I can remember one of my professors asking me why I was doing that. "Football stadiums aren't architecture," he told me. At the time it was seen as something that an engineer would do, but there wasn't any architecture in it. Most architects just didn't believe football stadiums were regarded as architecture, which I think shows what the attitudes were at that time.

'After university I came back here and was put on the Huddersfield project, commuting from Liverpool where I lived to Huddersfield where I worked on site.'

* * * *

Throughout the 1990s, and after Hillsborough and the subsequent demands of the Taylor Report that all top-level football grounds in England and Scotland should become all-seater, a period of great change took place at grounds across the country. In the 1980s, under-investment and neglect had caused many historic venues to crumble. They were dangerous and in some cases deadly. Post-Taylor, there would come renovated or new stands – the old terracing replaced by row after row of plastic seats – and in some cases entirely new stadiums. In all, it was a multi-million-pound nationwide building project that transformed grounds into safer and more comfortable arenas.

Between 1990 and 1999 a dozen new stadiums would be built by English league clubs – at Walsall, Chester, Millwall, Huddersfield, Northampton, Middlesbrough, Bolton, Derby, Stoke, Sunderland, Reading and Wigan. Of these, the project in Huddersfield stood out as the most impressive, showing the way as one of the most influential developments of the decade.

The Alfred McAlpine Stadium opened in the summer of 1994 with its futuristic and modern design. Bold and beautiful, bright and eye-catching, it sat in a dominant position in the landscape of the northern mill town. In the book, *All Points North*, a collection of writings on life and work, music and sport by the local poet Simon Armitage, he described it as 'looking like a blue and white lunar module'.

'[W]e do not build exciting modern stadia in this country,' the author and stadium expert Simon Inglis would write after it opened, 'certainly not in places like Huddersfield.'

* * * *

With its Archibald Leitch-designed Main Stand, Huddersfield Town's old Leeds Road had been a fine example of the traditional English football ground. It was located in the town and over the years had held record crowds of 60,000-plus to watch their First Division championship-winning teams (in the 1920s Town won three in a row). The club had had the great and innovative manager Herbert Chapman and later, before he arrived in Liverpool, Bill Shankly. By the late 1980s, though, tight finances at the club had meant that upkeep had lapsed as some areas grew tired and fell into disrepair. There were trough-like toilets for the gents and big puddles in the car park when it rained. Restrictions had been placed on the ground's capacity – average attendances in the early 1990s had ranged from just 5,500 to 7,500. Leeds Road was another crumbling English football home. The view from the club was that something better, newer and safer was needed.

At the Lobb Partnership in London they had been devising a new, post-Hillsborough concept for the future of stadium design. Lobb had already worked on a few football, rugby and horse-racing stands and, at an exhibition in Birmingham in 1991, they unveiled the concept design, 'A Stadium for the 90s'. It was a forward-thinking design for a stadium with arching, blue-roofed stands with clear sight lines of the playing surface for spectators, a strong vision of a new way forward in the field, an antidote to what had become a landscape of decay. The Huddersfield Town hierarchy were impressed by Lobb's design and boldly opted to progress with their plan.

In 1983 Simon Inglis released his great work, *Football Grounds of Britain*. On a shelf at home is the third edition (which came out in 1996). At his home in West Hampstead, north London, up in his study, are four walls of bookshelves filled with stadium books: English, French, Italian … Soviet. From his files he finds me a pack on Huddersfield that includes newspaper clippings and brochures for both the completed stadium and the original project concept. We sit and talk about stadium developments in the 1990s, Huddersfield's new ground and the project's influence thereafter.

'When I saw it, I really liked it,' recalls Inglis of his first view of the 'A Stadium for the 90s' design. It was a blueprint, a sort of a blue-sky thinking design. 'The cynical side of me would have said they haven't a hope, far too adventurous, who's going to take that one up? I can't remember exactly what I thought at the time seeing it – it was a long time ago now – but I'm pretty sure it would have been something like, "Good luck to them, but this is going to be tough."

'The idea of the spanning white truss to hold up the roof was nothing new. In technical terms it's an established method used to support or bear large spans and roofs. But to express it here in a curve and to articulate each detail of the steelwork as it resolves at ground level was to me a demonstration of engineering as artistry.'

In the words of Rod Sheard, one of the chief architects at Lobb, the aim for the Huddersfield project was to create 'a versatile sports, entertainment and hospitality facility, with a commercial theme integrated into the design … A futuristic stadium for the ultimate benefit of supporters of football and rugby league, the business sector and everyone who lives in the Kirkless community … a blueprint for others to follow.'

In 1992 planning permission was granted for the new stadium, which was to be located only a short distance away from Leeds Road on a derelict former chemical works site beside the River Colne. It would be built into a wooded hill, Kilner Bank, and Town and Huddersfield Giants Rugby League club would be joint tenants.

During 1993 and 1994, the stadium rose from the ground and on matchdays some fans would make the short walk over from Leeds Road to take a look at how things were progressing. As Inglis would write of its progress, 'Clearly visible from the old terraces, the steelwork rose up beyond the car park like the sun over the horizon.'

* * * *

'I do think that Huddersfield broke the mould, certainly in this country,' says Dale Jennins back at Populous. 'It was a very forward-thinking image of what could be done at a sensible price. It was an opportunity to create something unique and the project contained a great architectural vision that I think was required at the time. When the ground was being built up, a colleague and I used to go to the back of the stand and we'd look around, watching it developing, sort of out of the ground. It was a great time for me.'

The £15m final cost of the project was funded by £5m raised from the sale of the Leeds Road site, £3.75m from private investment, £4.25m in grants and £2m from the local council. Initially just two stands would be built along each side of the pitch, followed by a third behind one goal. The fourth, behind the opposite goal, would be finished a few years later eventually giving the stadium its 24,500 capacity.

'The language of the design was developed from three things,' explains Jennins. 'First, the concept of "A Stadium for the 90s". Then the site's location, in terms of all the hills behind it and everything. Then the strong colours of the cladding and the roofs and the seating [predominantly bold blue and white, red and yellow], which largely came from the fact it would be used by clubs from two different sports, football and rugby league. I suppose that was a fashion point also. At the time bright primary colours were in vogue and it was done in the architectural language of the late 80s and early 90s that was to kind of smack you in the face. It wasn't exactly a subtle time, but it was fun.

'In terms of some of the details, there were the white supports and the trusses and the "quadrapods" in the corner [where the trusses crossed and planted into the ground, holding the roof in place and providing a base for the floodlights]. I was involved in those bits. My own little thing was the control room in the corner.

'The impact of the large arches is the main thing. You see them coming down from the railway station and coming in on the train. The form of the curves and the crescent shapes that bring the seats as close to the centre of the pitch as possible created a form itself, the arched structure. A lot of that came from the original concept design.

'As a football supporter, I think its location is fantastic. I'd actually forgotten how good it was. But going to the Spurs match with a colleague there [in 2017] and walking down from the station past the old market was just a great experience. I think that all stadiums that have a relationship with the centre of a town or a city are important, Newcastle probably being the best for that. Huddersfield is definitely one of them as well and that's important, I think.'

* * * *

After it opened in 1994, Rod Sheard would hail the new stadium a 'landmark' venue and 'dramatic building whose strong curves and colours stand out starkly against the surrounding wooded slopes and the grey tones of most of Huddersfield's townscape'.

'I loved it,' says Inglis, 'absolutely loved it. I remember kind of thinking, "Blimey, it's a bit curvy for a start." Certainly eye-catching. They used contrasting bright blue and white cladding. You could look down on it from the hills above and see that it was special. The way they finished it showed that someone had actually thought through the whole design process. For me it was often difficult to write about stadium architecture, particularly when so many of the new examples were yet more iterations of the standard tin-shed approach. So this was a bit of a breath of fresh air.'

In 1995 recognition would come in the form of the Royal Institute of British Architects' (RIBA) Building of the Year award. For Dale Jennins, who years before at university had been told that 'football stadiums weren't architecture', the award represented quite a progression in the field. 'The RIBA award certainly vindicated what we were doing and what I believed,' he says, 'which was that stadium design could be good architecture. I'd felt confident that that was the case anyway. But with that award it showed that thoughts and ideas had changed dramatically.'

The last match at the old Leeds Road ground came in April 1994, a 2-1 win for Town against Blackpool in the Second Division. It was an emotional day for the club's supporters, saying goodbye to a fond old friend, the club's home since 1908. Afterwards some fans removed pieces of turf from the pitch as mementos. Then the bulldozers moved in to make way for a new retail park.

The first home league game in the new stadium came at the start of the 1994/95 season. Some 13,000 were there for the first time to experience this fine post-Taylor Report arena of 'New' football.

A Sacred Place

Near to Huddersfield is the village of Mirfield where the Town fan John Robb has kindly invited me into his home. Robb, a retired teacher, attended his first Town game in 1950 and has loyally followed the club ever since. For 18 years, he was secretary of the Heavy Woollen branch of Town's supporters' club (Heavy Woollen, including towns like Heckmondwike, Dewsbury, Batley and Mirfield, being the district of West Yorkshire known for producing heavyweight cloth). To date, he has visited 120-plus different grounds watching his team, every visit to a new ground neatly logged in a small notebook. Sitting in his conservatory, with him wearing a Huddersfield Town jumper and me drinking tea from one of his Town mugs, he talks me through a life supporting the club.

'To begin with myself and my dad would go to the game on the bus into town. Then when I was about 13 or 14, I used to go on my own on my bike and park it outside one of the houses behind the ground. I used to take my haversack, duffel bag, whatever, with books and pictures in it and I'd go down to the players' entrance to get their autographs. They were marvellous those books, full of cuttings from papers and magazines. I had two full pages for each team in the top two divisions and took this enormous thing along with me to the matches. I had Stanley Matthews, Stan Mortensen, Nat Lofthouse, Bobby Charlton. Over the years they've disappeared, which is a real shame. The first year I really started going was the 1952/53 season when we got promoted from the Second Division. That was a super season. When Bill Shankly was with us [1956–59]. We were back in the Second Division. Obviously he was a great figure even before he went to Liverpool, a great character.

'We had reasonably good crowds at Leeds Road [around 15,000 through the Shankly years] and it was a good atmosphere for the games. I used to stand on the large stand on the side, not behind the goals. I was about three-quarters of the way to the back, level with the penalty area. I loved the old ground. In fact, I didn't want to leave it for the new stadium when we were moving. But I suppose it did need to change and a great deal of money would have to have been spent to bring it up to standard.'

Robb can remember the last day at Leeds Road in 1994, saying goodbye to the old place and the fans piling on to the pitch at the end. 'How many thousands got on there? It was the last match and we won against Blackpool. I must say, though, as soon as I walked into the new stadium I was totally hooked. It felt like home straight away. And of course I had a seat now rather than being stood up.'

In his book, *Sport, Space and the City*, the academic John Bale writes of the importance of a stadium's location, its attachment to an area; how it can be 'a sacred place … a home'. There is, then, much to be said for keeping a stadium close to its roots and its heart, close to the people who support the team that plays there. When they built their new stadium in the 1990s, Huddersfield managed to do that, kept it near to and part of the community, visible to the people who live there.

For John Robb, his matchday routine didn't change much as the club moved from its old ground to the new stadium. 'I still leave the house at the same time as I used to. I pick two friends up at 1.30pm, just in case there's traffic and queues, then we drive the long way round and park at around 2pm. Sometimes we walk all the way round the ground to see if there is anything going on near the shop and the entrance, then we go to our seats and watch the players warm up. Nothing much else has really changed from the old days. My seat is in the same place as where I used to stand at Leeds Road, level with the penalty area, three-quarters of the way back. Just like where we were before, where we've always been. I love it.'

* * * *

In the 1990s, after a bright blue-and-white statement of progress had been dropped in the middle of the Yorkshire town, Huddersfield's new home helped change the landscape for stadium design in this country. No longer were there fences or standing terraces; dilapidation and danger were gone too. A new standard had been set.

A later development from Lobb was the Reebok Stadium in Bolton. With its curving roof, clear sight lines, futuristic and interesting look, it took its lead from Huddersfield, the next in line in the evolution of new stadium design. Jennins was involved in that project. 'Bolton was an evolution from Huddersfield,' he explains. 'There is a direct link.

'Looking back generally, I think that Huddersfield certainly changed the attitudes about stadiums amongst architects. With the likes of Foster & Partners who we worked with at Wembley, the kind of architects who want to work on football stadiums now, looking back to the 80s, probably wouldn't have touched them with a bargepole. But Huddersfield, then Bolton, completely changed the concept of football stadiums as architecture.'

In 1995, Middlesbrough opened their rectangular Riverside Stadium to replace Ayresome Park. In 1997, there was Pride Park in Derby, replacing the Baseball Ground. With their standard-looking form they were pretty similar. The same could be said for the others that followed in Stoke (1997), Southampton (2001) and Leicester (2002). The Stadium of Light in Sunderland, replacing Roker Park in 1997, was larger but also had similarities.

'Don't get me wrong, they are all perfectly adequate and good stadiums technically,' says Jennins. 'They're all comfortable and safe. But with Huddersfield, then Bolton, we were trying to create something unique and iconic.'

Throughout the 1990s the publisher Ian Allan produced its *Aerofilms Guide* to football stadiums series – a collection of aerial photos of the football grounds in the country that it released every season. Chronicled in alphabetical order by club, the books feature the photos and stats (such as attendance records), current capacity and information on future potential developments of the grounds. Looking through each edition you can track the evolution of the grounds through the decade – new stands or new stadiums being built to replace the old and dilapidated structures. The first copy I had was the fourth edition, from 1996. Inside were all of the great places which, apart from Hillsborough, I'd never been to or even seen in person. St James', Villa and Goodison Park, Wembley, Anfield and Old Trafford. Roker Park in Sunderland and Burnden Park in Bolton were still there. Huddersfield's, with its striking bright blue roof, was there. By the sixth edition in 1997, the half-built new stadiums in Bolton, Derby, Stoke and Sunderland were there as well.

After Huddersfield and Bolton, Jennins was involved in the new Wembley. Then he was architect for the new Tottenham Hotspur stadium project – with its 62,000 capacity, the shiniest and sleekest and glassiest and best of all the new stadiums.

'Probably the big difference with the Tottenham stadium is obviously that the finances available are different,' he says. 'Architecturally you have more scope in terms of what you can do. There's more money available nowadays and stadiums now are more of a destination, particularly in terms of what you can do on non-match days. You know, years ago you didn't really necessarily think hugely about non-match day elements, but this will be an all-singing, all-dancing thing in terms of what you can do with your stadium, how it can operate all year round. I think that it's changing the perception of what a stadium is today. And I do think that goes back to Huddersfield.'

Premier Town

November 2017. I'm in town to watch Huddersfield v West Bromwich Albion in the Premier League.

Framed by the Pennine hills that roll around it, its larger neighbours Manchester sat in one direction and Leeds in the other, Huddersfield is a fine old manufacturing town where old textile mills still stand (though perhaps now are converted to flats or similar). The town has a multicultural population: around 15 per cent of its 150,000-plus inhabitants are of Asian origin, for instance. Its university is vibrant and punches above its weight nationally. The annual Contemporary Music Festival is world renowned.

Some people here wear flat caps, and they like their football and rugby league.

Huddersfield's industrial past produced prosperity and wealth, which brought handsome architecture and the Victorian buildings for which it was once acclaimed. The station (built in 1850), with its imposing columns by the entrance, sets a grand scene on arrival. The nearby George Hotel (also opened in 1850 and the birthplace of rugby league) is closed and in need of some love.

At the station is the statue of Harold Wilson, who seems to be about to stride off down the hill, perhaps towards the football. Wilson was twice Prime Minister of the country in the 1960s and 1970s and grew up here. On more successful days his statue has been known to have blue-and-white Huddersfield Town scarves tied around its neck. Wilson loved his football. 'The great treat of the week was to be allowed to go and watch Huddersfield Town playing during their great days,' he explained in his memoirs. 'I would leave home at about 10am. My mother would give me a shilling. The number 4 tram from Marsden to Bradley went through the town right to the ground and cost one penny each way. Entrance was sixpence, the programme cost twopence … When Huddersfield Town won the league championship three years running and the [FA] Cup Final in two of those years, we felt we were the Lords of Creation.'

He liked a good football-politics analogy or two as well. On leading the country and, specifically, managing his cabinet, he referred to his role as the 'deep-lying centre-half', the co-ordinator and orchestrator of the team. On political setbacks, 'I had mine when I was relegated in 1970. You know, when we lost the election.'

Today there are already fans wandering around town with their blue-and-white-striped Town shirts.

My friend Pat has lived in the area for more than 15 years and we meet in a pub, The Sportsman, to catch up. We went to school together in Sheffield but now he lives in the village of Marsden, seven miles outside Huddersfield. He studied music at Huddersfield University and when he finished he didn't want to leave. After Town were promoted to the Premier League in 2017, the whole place was lifted. When they beat Manchester United 2-1 a few weeks ago, Pat sent me a text from the pub, 'Oh my god.'

'Huddersfield is an old industrial town,' he says. 'It's proud of its heritage. The mills and the factories and the buildings. And we're not a city, we're a town. But we're a big town and people from here love to remind you of that. They're proud of that.

'When they [Town] went up and it got to penalties at Wembley, you knew how important it was. It was definitely the most important moment I've seen since I've been here. When that final penalty went in, the pub we were in lifted up like a rocket, it was bonkers. People were jumping on tables and everything. I'm sure that things like that happen everywhere, but it was just ace. Everyone was just really happy.

'Now all of these big teams like Man Utd, Man City, Liverpool, will come to Huddersfield. There's this prestige of having these teams coming here. Sky matches, everything. The amount of people in town on a Saturday afternoon has definitely gone up. It's much busier. And the Premier League thing was plastered all over the train station – Premier Town. All of a sudden people knew where Huddersfield was. People who you never knew cared about football now seemed to care about football. It was bringing people together.

'Where the football ground is, it's an interesting bit of town. It's about the only thing down there. The ground is a kind of landmark. You can walk there easily, it's 15 minutes from up here. When there's a game on, it's a massive stream of fans going down there. Everyone walks. From the station down to the ground, it's a continuous line of people. It's great really.'

Later, I leave Pat in the pub and make my way to the ground, walking down the hill by the town's outdoor market (opened in 1889, with its cast-iron columns). Farther on I join Leeds Road and the white arches and floodlights of the stadium come into view, Kilner Bank rising behind. To the left along the road is the retail park where the old ground once stood. I cross the canal and walk past the rusting gasometers of the old gasworks before the John Smith's stadium comes into view: the bright blue curved roofs and white arches of the swooping and compact modern stadium.

* * * *

In 2016/17, Huddersfield achieved their remarkable promotion from the Championship to the Premier League. They were led there by their German coach David Wagner, once Jurgen Klopp's reserve team manager at Borussia Dortmund, who built a close-knit and hard-working side that punched well above its financial weight. The season they were promoted, Huddersfield had one of the lowest wage bills in the Championship.

Wagner was appointed by Dean Hoyle, the club's millionaire owner who made his fortune with the greetings card retail chain Card Factory. Hoyle is a big Town fan and had gone to Leeds Road before moving on to the seats of the new stadium. When the club was still in the Championship, many fans had committed to season tickets and backed the club when Hoyle asked them to. When they reached the Premier League, they were thanked with £100 season tickets (the full price would be just £199) – Premier League football at Yorkshire prices. 'I'm a custodian of fans' dreams,' Hoyle had said of his role with the club. Only six seasons earlier the club was in League Two, the fourth tier of English football.

It's still a while before kick-off but there is a crowd around the players' entrance. I nip into the club shop and buy a David Wagner mug and a Town-branded flat cap. In the window there is a poster that reads, 'Our spirit is what makes us different'.

I've been here a number of times before to watch Sheffield Wednesday and have had good and bad days. I'm meeting up with a friend whose spare season ticket I'm borrowing for the afternoon. Inside the stadium we have a good view, just up and across from the dugouts. The stadium looks super today. It's still looking futuristic and definitely fit for the top level even 20-plus years after its construction.

Just before half-time the Dutch forward Rajiv van La Parra bends in a great strike past Ben Foster in the West Brom goal to make it 1-0 to Town. The stadium erupts. As the afternoon draws on and the sky darkens on the trees behind the stand, they turn to silhouette against the now bright floodlights. Wagner, with his glasses and baseball cap, jumps up and down on the touchline to stir up the crowd for the final push. They hold on for the win. By the end of the season, Huddersfield will achieve their hard-fought survival. It will mean a second year in the Premier League, albeit one that ultimately ends in relegation.

As the club has climbed and fallen through the top few divisions since its construction in 1994, their stadium has stood there through it all, remaining a significant symbol of the club and part of the fabric of the town. For Dale Jennins at Populous there is satisfaction when looking back at the Huddersfield project, particularly when considering its enduring legacy and influence upon what followed. 'When I went back, I was amazed at how it has lasted and how fresh it still looks. I think it works really well. The atmosphere when I was there was very good, too. The proximity of everyone to the pitch and the acoustics, the shape of the stadium, all help that. All these years on and it still good, I think, compared to other stadiums. It was designed to be a Premier League stadium, to take Huddersfield to the next level. Seeing it up there I think vindicated what we had been trying to achieve.'

5

Football's Coming Home

IN THE 1990s there was war on Europe's doorstep as the nation of Yugoslavia broke apart. With four major conflicts across the Balkans – Serbia-Slovenia, Serbia-Croatia, Serbia-Croatia-Bosnia (in Bosnia) and, later, Kosovo-Bosnia – the region was brutally divided. Millions of people were displaced, there was barbaric ethnic cleansing and over a hundred thousand people lost their lives.

'Back in 1991, it became clear that Yugoslavia was breaking up as the country accelerated to disaster,' wrote the journalist and broadcaster Tim Marshall in his first-hand account of the conflict, *Shadowplay: Behind the Lines & Under Fire – The Inside Story of Europe's Last War*. 'After losing Slovenia, Serbia's President Slobodan Milosevic unleashed the might of the Serb-dominated military on to first Croatia and then Bosnia and Herzegovina to prevent them from following.'

'It's like the photographs of German cities in 1945, except in colour and 3D,' Timothy Garton Ash would note of what he saw in his book, *History of the Present: Essays, Sketches and Despatches from Europe in the 1990s*.

Throughout the decade there would be NATO interventions and bombing campaigns, then the downfall of Serbian leader Slobodan Milosevic and the creation of several new nations.

One of these new nations had a new football team. Playing in red-and-white tablecloth checked strips, Croatia were admitted to FIFA in 1992 and boasted an incredibly talented group of players. They had the uncompromising defenders Igor Stimac and Slaven Bilic, the elegant midfielders Robert Prosinecki and Zvonimir Boban, and the supremely gifted strikers Alen Boksic and Davor Suker. Several of this group had previously represented the Yugoslavia national team. Now they wore the Croatia shirt with pride and carried with them a deep sense of responsibility for their people when they did.

Stimac signed for Derby County in 1995 and would explain what playing for his country meant to him, 'It makes me very happy. I can't explain, it's something special, it's some responsibility … I just feel like I can't lose the game, because it's not about money, it's not football – it's a fight for your country … We are a new country, a small country … our people was dying … we spent five years in a war for nothing. So the football team is very important.'

In the summer of 1996, Croatia came to England to compete in their first international tournament after gliding through their qualification matches unbeaten.

* * * *

Euro 96 was the first major footballing tournament to be held in England since the World Cup in 1966. In Sheffield, Hillsborough stadium was to host three group stage matches with Croatia playing in one of them. I was about 11 at the time and my dad got us two tickets for the Denmark-Croatia game on the first Sunday of the tournament. I'd had no idea that he'd got them and had settled for watching all of the games on TV. But now we were going to the game.

We walked down the hill to the ground and Dad bought me a programme. It had a bright orange cover and information on the four teams in Group D: this featured new nation Croatia; Denmark, whose friendly supporters took over the Kop at Hillsborough and played football with locals in the nearby park. In the city they drank pubs dry and in an outdoor shopping precinct worshipped a giant mechanical clock; Turkey; and finally Portugal – the story goes that some of their fans visited the fans' embassy in Sheffield to ask about the whereabouts of the beach. I still have the programme and our ticket stubs from the game (£25 each, even for juniors).

Our seats were in the Croatia end and, as my dad reminds me, their fans were pretty boisterous, having a great time watching their new team. That day Peter Schmeichel was beaten three times in the Denmark goal, twice by the superb Suker. For his second, he produced one of the best things I've seen live at a football game when he chipped Schmeichel from inside the area, over his head and into the net.

* * * *

Back in late 1991, the Football Association had made its bid to host Euro 96. English clubs had served their post-Heysel European ban, the stadiums had been developed and here was an opportunity to put England and English football back on centre stage. It was the next step in its domestic renaissance and international re-emergence. In May 1992, UEFA announced that the FA's bid had been successful and president Lennart Johansson proclaimed, 'Their national game has been re-accepted.'

The threat of hooliganism on home soil was still a potential problem, however. In the years leading up to Euro 96, there had been incidents of bad behaviour from England fans following their country abroad. At Euro 88 in West Germany, of the 823 people that had been arrested during the tournament 381 were English fans. At Euro 92 in Sweden, there had been trouble in Malmo and Stockholm when England were in town. In 1993 hundreds of England fans were arrested and deported from Holland after disturbances in Rotterdam before a World Cup qualifier. Then in 1995, there was England's game against the Republic of Ireland in Dublin which was cut short and abandoned after hooligans tore up and threw wooden seats from their stand at Lansdowne Road. Although violence was in general becoming a decreasing blight on the game, particularly at the grounds themselves – and certainly when compared to events of the 80s – it still had by no means disappeared.

After the events in Sweden in 1992 Johansson had commented less positively of English football, 'This cannot go on year after year… the English government and the FA need to reconsider the situation and see what they can do about the future.'

Nevertheless, in 1996 the matches would take place at Wembley Stadium, Villa Park (Birmingham), Anfield (Liverpool), St James' Park (Newcastle), Old Trafford (Manchester), Elland Road (Leeds), the City Ground

(Nottingham) and Hillsborough (Sheffield). Wembley and the Premier League grounds were now all-seater, either refurbished or with new stands built, like at Old Trafford and St James'.

For the three-week spectacle, three were 16 nations in England. The big hitters, Italy, France, the Netherlands, Germany and Spain, would be there. They were joined by Scotland, Switzerland, Czech Republic, Russia, Belgium and Romania, Group D's Croatia, Denmark, Turkey and Portugal, and the hosts.

Today, leafing through a nearly complete Euro 96 Merlin sticker album, price £1 and with its shiny cover and colourful graphics on each page, I find all of the star players from the competing nations inside. From the Premier League clubs, there are most of the England squad and some of Scotland's, along with figures like Andrei Kanchelskis (Everton and Russia), Peter Schmeichel (Manchester Utd and Denmark) and Dan Petrescu (Chelsea and Romania). From farther afield, the Netherlands manager Guus Hiddink (complete with his moustache), Jurgen Klinsmann (Germany), Gianfranco Zola and Paolo Maldini (Italy), Michael and Brian Laudrup (Denmark), plus the heroes of the USA 94 Hristo Stoichkov (Bulgaria) and Gheorghe Hagi (Romania).

* * * *

Back at Euro 92, Graham Taylor's England had failed miserably as they exited the competition at the group stage. They hadn't even qualified for USA 94 and Taylor left in 1993, 'Do I not like that' ringing loud. He was replaced by Terry Venables who would lead England at Euro 96.

Venables had played for Chelsea, Tottenham and Queens Park Rangers in the 1960s and 1970s. As coach he had taken Barcelona to the European Cup Final in 1986 and later won the FA Cup with Tottenham before being sacked by the Spurs owner Alan Sugar in 1993 (Sugar, whose Amstrad company made the satellite dishes for Sky TV, had been unhappy over Venables's business dealings; in 1998, Venables would be disqualified for seven years by the High Court from acting as a company director).

After the disappointing Taylor era, Venables was seen as a fresh new way forward for the national side and would encourage an attractive modern brand of football that would resuscitate England.

His squad for Euro 96 had a strong make-up of Manchester United, Newcastle United, Liverpool and Arsenal players, with almost half of his 22-man selection playing for those clubs. Among them were Gary and Phil Neville (Manchester United); Les Ferdinand and Steve Howey (Newcastle); Steve McManaman, Robbie Fowler and Jamie Redknapp (Liverpool); David Seaman, Tony Adams and David Platt (Arsenal). Added to these were Paul Gascoigne (by now playing for Glasgow Rangers following his £4.3m move from Lazio the previous summer), Gareth Southgate (Aston Villa), Stuart Pearce (Nottingham Forest), Paul Ince (Inter Milan), Teddy Sheringham and Darren Anderton (Tottenham), and Alan Shearer (Blackburn Rovers).

England's preparations had taken the group on a controversial tour of the Far East where they played games against China in Beijing then in Hong Kong against a 'Golden Select XI'. On a night out in Hong Kong some of the players decided to get shit-faced drunk, and for some of them their night would involve a 'Dentist's Chair' experience where a variety of alcoholic shots were delivered down the international footballers' necks – Gascoigne was among the participants. On the flight back to England, Gascoigne, drunk again, caused £5,000 of damage to the plane and back home the tabloid newspapers were scalding.

Despite this controversy, by the time of England's first game most of the attention returned to the pitch and the hopes of Venables's side. Their opener was against Switzerland at Wembley and on that first Saturday afternoon the old stadium was decked out with St George's flags waved around by the 76,000 crowd. Shearer put England ahead in the first half of what was a tight encounter, his first goal for his country for 12 games, but with seven minutes to go Switzerland pinned them back. The match finished 1-1 to make for a flat start for the hosts.

* * * *

Elsewhere in England, in Euro 96 City, Italy beat Russia in Liverpool, Croatia beat Turkey in Nottingham, France beat Romania in Newcastle and Bulgaria drew with Spain in Leeds (initially, Bulgaria were based on the North Yorkshire coastal town of Scarborough but, bored with their designated base, left for the party town of Stockton).

Despite the enthusiasm for England at Wembley, attendances at some of the other venues turned out lower than hoped for by the organisers. In Newcastle, Bulgaria-Romania attracted just 19,000. Russia-Czech Republic at Anfield drew 21,000. Denmark-Turkey in Nottingham saw just 19,000 turn up. Possibly this was down to the cost of the tickets, which were priced between £15 and £45 for the group games at a time when the average price of a Premier League ticket was around £13. There were better crowds in Manchester at Old Trafford, though, (50,000-plus for Russia-Germany and Italy-Germany) and in Birmingham at Villa Park (34,000-plus for Scotland-Netherlands and Switzerland-Netherlands).

A week after Switzerland, Scotland were next up for England. Earlier that day, the IRA had exploded a bomb in the centre of Manchester, causing extensive damage to many buildings in the city. Over 50,000 were due at Old Trafford on the Sunday for the Russia-Germany game and, despite the chaos the bomb had caused, it was decided that both the England-Scotland game at Wembley later that day and the Manchester game the day after would go ahead as planned.

This was England and Scotland's first meeting since 1989 and would be settled by two key moments in a single second-half minute of play.

First, after Shearer had earlier put England ahead, Scotland won a penalty after Adams had brought down Gordon Durie in the area. Gary McAllister stepped up. His strike was strong and to the right, but Seaman managed to deny him with his elbow. England then broke upfield and Sheringham found Anderton who knocked it over first time towards Gascoigne. With the ball in his path he flicked it over Blackburn defender Colin Hendry before striking it on the volley into the net. The goal, which would secure England's 2-0 win, would become one of the iconic moments of Euro 96 – as would his Hong Kong dentist chair-esque celebration: with bleach blond hair, Gazza slid on his back for Sheringham to squirt water at him from a nearby drinks bottle.

England had won and as the St George's flags waved at Wembley again, momentum was beginning to build for Venables's side.

* * * *

The soundtrack to that summer's football was provided by the comedians Frank Skinner and David Baddiel, and the Liverpool band the Lightning Seeds. As the tournament went on and England progressed, their track 'Three Lions', with its famous 'Football's coming home' line, became ever more anthemic. The song reached number one in the charts and would be sung out loud by the Wembley crowd at the England games.

Baddiel and Skinner hosted the football show, *Fantasy Football League*, a shambolic and irreverent look at the game presented from a mock living-room television studio set. Complete with brown sofa (the IKEA revolution having yet to fully take hold in the country) and football memorabilia, the show was filmed in front of a boisterous group of football fans. It featured funny segments and footballing in-jokes. Each episode they'd do things like say 'Hello' to a football celebrity – 'This week we'll be saying a big hello to Billy Bremner ... "Hello!"' They'd recreate famous footballing moments in 'Phoenix from the Flames' and at the end of episodes the former West Bromwich Albion hero Jeff Astle would sing a song.

Baddiel and Skinner and *Fantasy Football* could be grouped as part of the cultural movement that was taking place in the country in the middle of the 90s; the term 'Cool Britannia' providing a neat wrap-around label for various exciting things that were happening around that time. In music this covered 'Britpop', led by the bands Oasis, Blur and Pulp. Popular films included *Trainspotting* and *Four Weddings and a Funeral*. And the 'Young British Artists' generation featured Damien Hirst, who'd created his famous shark-in-formaldehyde piece. In comedy there were programmes like *Father Ted*, *Shooting Stars* and *The Fast Show*. As Oasis's Noel Gallagher would later reflect of the time, 'We were all young, opinionated, talented and cool.'

There was also *Loaded*, the lairy glossy magazine 'for men who should know better'. *Loaded* was launched in 1995 and was aimed at 'lads' who did drinking and looked at 'birds' with not too many clothes on.

* * * *

Back at Wembley for their third game of the tournament, England faced the Netherlands who would pose Venables's side with their biggest test of Euro 96 so far.

Lining up in their orange shirts and white shorts, the Dutch team included several players from Louis van Gaal's exciting Ajax group. Ajax had won the Champions League in 1995, beating AC Milan 1-0 in Vienna through a late Patrick Kluivert strike. A year later, just weeks before Euro 96, they had reached the final again though this time lost to Juventus on penalties in Rome.

Van Gaal had nurtured a superb generation of gifted and highly technical players, including Kluivert, the de Boer twins (Ronald and Frank), Clarence Seedorf, Winston Bogarde, Michael Reiziger, goalkeeper Edwin van der Sar and Edgar Davids. Although Davids had been thrown out of the Dutch camp because of a fall-out with Dutch coach Guus Hiddink, and Frank de Boer was injured, the rest of that group formed the core of the Netherlands side. Going into the tournament they had been favourites to win it.

At Wembley, however, England shone as they brilliantly brushed aside the Dutch 4-1 to advance to the quarter-final.

After 23 minutes Shearer had put England 1-0 ahead with a penalty, before Sheringham's header from a Gascoigne corner later made it 2-0. The third brought a wonderful moment with Gascoigne cutting back to Sheringham in the box, whose disguised side-pass found Shearer who blasted it past van der Sar – an excellent goal for Venables's team. For 4-0 it was Sheringham again, before Kluivert rallied late on for the Netherlands' consolation.

Wembley bounced and 'Three Lions' rang round. It was one of the best England performances for years, showing up the fancied Dutch with their own superb style of play. 'England gave us a lesson in every department,' Hiddink would say afterwards.

For England's quarter-final, again at Wembley, Spain were unfortunate not to progress past the hosts as they were denied two good penalty calls and had a goal wrongly ruled out for offside. Extra time would follow the goalless 90 minutes and with no breakthrough made by either side, penalties were needed to decide things.

England's exit from Italia 90 to West Germany had come via this cruel, tie-breaking drama, Chris Waddle's skied penalty having denied them a place in the World Cup Final that time around. In Turin, Stuart Pearce had also failed to convert when his penalty was saved. In 1996, he stepped up bravely against Spain and powerfully put away his attempt. His celebration was a great outpouring of emotion, of clenched fists and screaming, as he exorcised the pain of his miss six years previously. England won the shoot-out, Pearce was redeemed and Wembley bounced again.

Elsewhere, in Euro 96's other quarter-finals, the Czech Republic beat Portugal 1-0 at Villa Park, Karel Poborsky's magnificent lobbed goal sending his country through. After the tournament Poborsky would be on his way to the Premier League and Manchester United (as would his Czech team-mate Patrik Berger who joined Liverpool). At Anfield France defeated the still fancied Dutch team on penalties, while in Manchester Germany beat Croatia 2-1. For the Croatian fans we'd seen in Sheffield, although their party was over their team had done their country proud with the excellent football they played. In the semi-finals the Czech Republic would beat France at Old Trafford on penalties. England, meanwhile, would take on the Germans.

* * * *

The last meeting in a major international competition between England and Germany (then still West Germany) had come in Turin in 1990, and it was now 30 years since the World Cup Final of '66 and England's 4-2 victory over them at Wembley.

In '96, anticipation in the country had been growing with each step England took through the tournament. Naturally, the Germany game was built up to extreme heights, particularly by the media and especially the tabloids – the red-tops stoking it up with various references to the Second World War as the game approached. '*Mirror* declares football war on Germany', read that paper's front page beside the headline 'ACHTUNG! SURRENDER', plus the sub-header, 'For you Fritz, ze Euro 96 Championship is over.'

'[L]et's not spoil it,' Venables would comment of the coverage.

* * * *

On that warm summer's evening the huge Wembley crowd again looked magnificent, waving their St George's flags. 'You'll Never Walk Alone', usually played at Anfield before Liverpool games, blared out. So did 'Three Lions'. Was this England's time?

Germany would play in their white tops and black shorts and England in their 'indigo blue' change strip (designed by Jeff Banks and which actually looked more like grey). More than 20 million people were watching on television and England lined up strong: Seaman; Adams, Southgate, Pearce; Anderton, Platt, Ince, McManaman, Gascoigne; Shearer and Sheringham.

It took just three minutes for the hosts to take the lead when Shearer, again, headed in from Gascoigne's cross for his fifth goal of the tournament. It was a great start, but it was too early to get carried away. On 16 minutes, Stefan Kuntz equalised for Germany and the game became deadlocked.

In extra time, England had their chances to win it. Anderton first hit the post – a great opportunity. Then came Gascoigne's moment. As the ball was played across the box by Shearer, Gazza stretched towards an open goal but missed his connection by only centimetres. Thanks to the newly introduced sudden-death golden goal rule for the tournament, had he been fractionally quicker off the mark he would have won it for England to send them through to the final.

After 120 minutes of battle and with no way through, it would be penalties again for England and Germany.

Germany struck away theirs efficiently and without mistake – five from five. But so did England as Shearer, Platt, Pearce, Gascoigne and Sheringham all netted. Then up stepped Gareth Southgate, and all the pressure was on the England defender's shoulders.

He ran up but struck tamely towards the corner of the goal. Andreas Kopke saved.

'All I can say is I'm sorry,' Southgate would later say of his miss.

Next up was Andreas Moller who buried his attempt high and handsome down the middle of the goal. Germany had won it and England were out. A great chance at glory had passed them by and a nation's hearts were broken. 'This team can look forward to the future with their heads held high,' Venables would reflect after the game. 'There is nothing to be downhearted about apart from the result.' In the final Germany would go on to beat the Czechs 2-1.

* * * *

After the tournament Venables left his post, the Football Association opting not to extend his contract and instead moving on to Chelsea's Glenn Hoddle. Hoddle would be tasked with building on the progress made under Venables, guiding what was a talented group of players to the World Cup in France in two years' time.

After the Germany game violence had broken out in central London at Trafalgar Square, and 200 people were arrested. It was the worst trouble in the capital since the poll tax riots of 1990. In Brighton, a Russian exchange student was stabbed five times in the neck after his accent was wrongly identified as German. Despite these events, in general the tournament had shown that English football could put together a successful and inclusive event on its own shores. Later, thoughts would turn to an ultimately unsuccessful bid for the 2006 World Cup.

Along with the exploits of the national side, Euro 96 would spur even more positive feelings for the game in the country, part of its continuing journey towards becoming an ever more mainstream and popular pastime. In the seasons that followed the tournament, total attendances in England would increase to 22.8m in 1996/97 (up from 21.9m in 1995/96) and to 24.7m in 1997/98, the highest levels since the late 70s. The number of women attending matches in England would increase as well (though proportionally women would still remain in the minority in the stadiums). Meanwhile, with each passing season, the number of overseas players playing in the Premier League would continue to rise, contributing to an ever more cosmopolitan make-up of the league.

In October 1996 at their party conference in Blackpool, the Labour leader Tony Blair would deliver a speech which featured lines that echoed the 'Three Lions' England song, 'Seventeen years of hurt never stopped us dreaming, Labour's coming home!' By the following May, he would be the country's new prime minister after beating John Major's Conservatives in a landslide General Election victory, taking 418 seats to their 165. Gone would be the long shadow of Thatcher-Major Tory rule in Britain. As Blair would say, 'A new dawn has broken, has it not?'

Two decades on from Euro 96 and his penalty miss, Gareth Southgate would take charge of the England national team and foster a team spirit and togetherness among his players, leading them to the semi-final of the 2018 World Cup in Russia. As for Paul Gascoigne, he would miss out on the World Cup in France in 1998. A troubled soul and flawed genius; life after the game would not be kind to him as battles with alcohol and depression sadly took a grip.

6

The Flickering Flame

Another Place

On the road again and west over those Pennine hills. Past
Manchester and 30 miles more to the great city on the water.
To Liverpool, the next great city of English football, for
meetings and a match. To be next to the water, the Mersey.

To set the scene and to get me ready I start with some
lines from Paul Du Noyer's *Liverpool: Wondrous Place*. 'It's
deeply insular,' he writes of his hometown, 'yet essentially
outward-looking: it faces the sea and all the lands beyond,
but has its back turned on England.'

Standing at the heart of the city's waterfront there
are 'The Three Graces', the trio of imposing buildings of
Liverpool's great sea-faring past, stood side-by-side and
facing out to the river and beyond. To the Irish Sea, the
Atlantic and the Americas. The world.

The largest of these is the Royal Liver Building, once
the headquarters of the Royal Liver Assurance group.
Topped by the city's Liver Bird symbol, for decades its four
clock faces have told the time of day to the people of the city
and the arriving ships. Next door is the Cunard Building,

former home to the Cunard Line transatlantic carrier. Beside that is the Port of Liverpool Building, previously the headquarters of the Mersey Docks and Harbour Board that manages the city's ports and docks. Near to the 'Graces' are the statues of the lads, The Beatles, walking along together and smiling. In 1995 they released a new song, 'Free as a Bird', built on a John Lennon demo and developed by the surviving band members Paul, George and Ringo.

With its vast system of docks, wharves and warehouses, at one time Liverpool had almost 40 per cent of the world's shipping passing through it and was regarded as the 'Second City of the British Empire.' It was here that millions of people that were making their way to new lives across the Atlantic passed through, the final stopping point on their journey to the New World. Of the five million that emigrated from Europe for America and Canada between 1819 and 1859, it is estimated that over two-thirds of them did so from Liverpool. Before that it had been the slave ships that headed first to the West African coast, where slaves were purchased, before being transported inhumanely across the Atlantic and then sold in the Caribbean. Between 1760 and 1807 (the year the trade was abolished in Great Britain), over 1,100 of these ships left the city.

Walking along the waterfront you come to the Albert Dock, the iconic brick warehouses turned tourist attraction that was renovated from ruin in the 1980s. Docks like this once employed thousands of Liverpool workers, whose job it was to load and unload cargo of ships from all over the world. As the decades passed, this industry shifted and changed and the emergence of larger container ships meant more cargo but fewer workers needed to work them. Increasing competition from

English and European ports compounded the challenges. In 1967, there were over 10,000 registered dockers in the city, but by 1989 this had fallen to just over 1,000, with many of the smaller docks all but abandoned. The car plants that had opened on the outskirts at Halewood (Ford) and upriver at Ellesmere Port (Vauxhall) would face their own turbulence.

In time the bustling docks that once lined the river would fade into a scene of abandonment and decay. Writing of the landscape he saw on his 1990s travels around England in *Yes We Have No: Adventures in Other England*, Nick Cohn observed (with similar conclusions to what he had seen at the shipyards of Newcastle), 'The docks and warehouses that teemed with work, the streets that never stopped roaring – they're half-deserted now … a wasteland.'

Later, I get back in the car and drive the miles along the old Dock Road myself, skirting the tall wall that demarks the road and the decay that lies behind it. Opposite Stanley Dock is the massive former tobacco warehouse, the world's largest brick building. At the Bramley-Moore Dock, Everton, the city's blue football club, plan to build a new stadium here to replace their Goodison Park home. Farther along the river is the Port of Liverpool with its stack upon stack of large shipping containers. Millions of tonnes of the world's cargo (over 30m) come through here every year, the port employing just a fraction of the workforce that had once been required.

Just beyond the port I arrive at windswept Crosby Beach where standing in the sand are 100 Antony Gormley cast-iron statues lining the beach. Placed here in 2005, they face out to the water and the world, their backs to the country. 'Another Place.'

* * * *

It's late February 2018 and the day after I arrive there's a Saturday afternoon kick-off for Liverpool FC, one of only seven of their league games to start at 3pm this season. The view from my hotel has the great wide river opposite and the imposing Liver Building to the left. Looking out of the windows feels like being at the front of a ship.

I walk up to the station and past the huge Soviet-style radio tower (standing tall since 1969) to pick up a taxi to Anfield. Each weekend the area is besieged by thousands and thousands of football fans converging here for the game, many of them visiting the city from other parts of the country and the world. Even hours before the match the area is bustling. I do the usual lap of the ground.

The new £114m three-tier Main Stand is a new giant on the skyline of Anfield. To make room for it, they knocked down three rows of houses behind it. Later on, up on its raised outside walkway, I'll watch the team bus drive past the fans before it descends into the stand. Nearby is the Hillsborough Memorial where the names of all 96 victims of that horrific day in 1989 are listed along with their ages. So many of the victims were so young: 16, 17, 18 years old.

Farther on is another huge Premier League megastore – two floors of replica shirts and mugs, cushions and Liverpool-branded vodka. Outside on the roads are the badge-sellers and food stalls. The Sandon pub where the club was founded in 1892 is packed to the rafters.

Outside the famous Kop – specifically, the new Kop that was completed in 1995, its 12,500 plastic seats having replaced the famous terrace where thousands more had once stood and swayed – is the statue of the great man

Bill Shankly. Two arms held aloft in triumph and a scarf around his bronze neck, Shankly was the architect of Liverpool's emergence in the 1960s. The man who awoke the sleeping giant, lifted them from the Second Division to the First, and built the foundations for the league titles and European adventures to follow. 'I was a man for the people,' said the man who all those years ago transformed the club. 'Everything I did was for the people.'

Simon Ellis-Jones works at the club and has organised a ticket for me in the Sir Kenny Dalglish Stand running along the side of the pitch. I pick it up and make my way round to my turnstile. Inside, there's no legroom but never mind.

The ground soon fills up and as kick-off approaches 'You'll Never Walk Alone' begins to play and the Anfield choir sings along. To my left, the 1990s Kop is a scene of waving flags and red-and-white scarves held above heads. In his programme notes for today's game, Liverpool's groovy German coach Jurgen Klopp talks about 'the mentality of being relentless'. Three days after taking Porto apart 5-0 in the Champions League, their swarming front three of Roberto Firmino, Sadio Mane and Mohamed Salah are in fine form as West Ham United are put away 4-1. There is a goal each for the devastating front trio, Liverpool's other 'Three Graces'. By May, Klopp's men will have reached Kiev and the Champions League Final. In two years, they'll be champions of England.

Mr Nice Guy

Throughout the 1970s and 1980s Liverpool were *the* dominant force in English football. After Bill Shankly (who won six major trophies with the club), there was

Bob Paisley, then Joe Fagan, then player-manager Kenny Dalglish. Between them, they guided the Reds to trophy after trophy. From 1975 (Paisley's first season in charge at Anfield) to 1990, their honours list read: ten First Division successes, two FA Cups, four League Cups and – chests out to the continent – one UEFA Cup and four European Cups.

Under Dalglish the dominance lasted until about 1989, the year of Hillsborough, after which the club began to lose its way. Dalglish left in 1991, the strain and stresses of the job compounded by the trauma of what he witnessed in Sheffield. Nobody at the time would have believed that Liverpool's First Division title win in 1989/90 would be the last the club would win for 30 years.

After Dalglish, the job was handed to Graeme Souness, Liverpool's successful captain of the 80s who had epitomised the dark hair, moustached and short shorts-wearing footballer of that era. As manager of Glasgow Rangers, Souness had led the Ibrox side to three Scottish league titles. At Liverpool, as football was changing from 'Old' to 'New', he sought to change and modernise the club. Attempts to influence improvements to player diet, for instance, were well intentioned – perhaps ahead of the curve in the very early 90s – but poorly executed. 'He tried to take on too much too soon,' one of his players would remember of his approach. 'He was very aggressive. He was having wars with everybody when he didn't need to, really ... If he'd gone in there with a feather instead of a sledgehammer, he might have been more successful.'

The players Souness brought to Anfield included Dunfermline's Hungarian midfielder Istvan Kozma (who played just six times), Danish defender Torben Piechnik (17 appearances) and West Ham's pragmatic left-back Julian

Dicks. But this was Liverpool, the leading English club of the past few decades, and signings like that simply didn't meet the standards of the past. As Manchester United were taking the nascent Premier League by storm, Liverpool drifted and in 1992/93 finished sixth.

In 1992 Souness underwent triple heart bypass surgery and afterwards he ill-advisedly sold his post-op interview to *The Sun*. The interview was considered deeply insensitive to the victims of the Hillsborough disaster and their families following the stories that that newspaper had printed in its aftermath – namely its 'THE TRUTH' headline and the false accusations of Liverpool fans stealing from victims as they lay on the pitch, and that they had assaulted police officers. To this day the boycott of *The Sun* continues on Merseyside and after his interview Souness's reputation in the city was markedly tarnished.

Through the 1993/94 season, attendances at Anfield averaged just below 36,000 and after First Division Bristol City knocked his Liverpool out of the FA Cup in January 1994, Souness resigned from his post. Promoted in his place was Roy Evans, a Liverpudlian who for almost 30 years had loyally served the club as both player and coach.

* * * *

Now aged 69, Evans has invited me to his house on the outskirts of the city to talk about his time in charge of the club in the 1990s. White-haired and clean-shaven, a top-class man who they used to call 'Mr Nice Guy', he greets me with a smile and a handshake.

'As a player I could have gone to Everton, Tottenham, Manchester United,' says Evans, settled down in his living

'My best moment? ... when I kicked the hooligan.' Manchester United's Eric Cantona, Selhurst Park 1995 [PA]

Wembley 1996. Cantona volleys home to win United the FA Cup [Getty]

USA 94. Brazil take to the field [Getty]

Italy's Roberto Baggio misses his World Cup Final penalty [Alamy]

Kevin Keegan looks on at his Newcastle United 'Entertainers', 1995 [PA]

Les Ferdinand scores against Everton at Goodison Park [Getty]

*'A Stadium
for the 90s',
Huddersfield*
[Ben Roberts]

[Colin
McPherson]

Euro 96. England fans outside Wembley [Alamy]

Alan Shearer and Teddy Sheringham celebrate another England goal against the Netherlands. It would finish 4-1 to the hosts [Alamy]

Croatia's Davor Suker at Hillsborough, Sheffield [Getty]

Solidarity. Robbie Fowler supports the Liverpool dockers, 1997 [Getty]

Tony Nelson (foreground) on the picket line, 1995 [Dave Sinclair]

France 98. Zinedine Zidane, Marseille [Getty]

Arsene Wenger celebrates Arsenal's Double, 1998 [PA]

'Football, bloody hell.' Manchester United complete the Treble, 1999 [PA]

room, 'but Liverpool was my club so I joined them in more or less 1965. I went right through the system and after a couple of years got through to the reserves. I hit a bit of brick wall trying to get into the first team because they were so good at the time [Evans would manage 11 appearances for the first team over the next few seasons].

'I was still only 25 when I was offered a job on the coaching staff. Shankly had just retired and Paisley had taken over and he offered me the job. I refused at first because obviously at that age I was being told something I didn't really want to hear – that I wasn't going to be making it into the team. But they asked me a few times and eventually I ended up taking it. They let me run the reserves as my team for almost ten years, pretty much how I wanted. After that I was first team coach for Joe Fagan, then assistant manager under Souness. I felt I'd done all the jobs and had a good idea about what was going on at the club.

'When Graeme left, I went round to the chairman's house [David Moores] and he offered me the job. I accepted of course. I didn't ask how much I would get paid or anything like that, I just said "Yes". When I got back home, that's when I started to get the enormity of it. I had all the responsibilities in my shoes now.'

With the club sitting fifth in the Premier League table, Evans had a job to do to bring Liverpool back to their former heights.

'Obviously over the years we were used to being a successful club. Graeme had come in and it hadn't quite gone right. He had some good ideas and obviously I was part of that as his assistant manager. But you've always got your own views and from that point I was able to put my own ideas into it.'

Key to Evans's philosophy was to get the team playing good, Liverpool football again.

'I wouldn't say that we had moved that far away from it. Shankly had the view that simplicity was genius and I think that that really worked. Other things like pass to the nearest red shirt were good ideas too. It was all about keeping the ball while people were trying to move and get into different areas of the pitch. Pass and move. So I tried to bring us back to that.'

In 1993/94, Evans would guide Liverpool to an eighth-placed finish in the Premier League and the season after was able to put more of a stamp on things. In came the defenders John Scales (£3.5m from Wimbledon) and Phil Babb (£3.6m from Coventry City). Out went midfielder Don Hutchison and the Souness signings Dicks and Piechnik. 'Graeme had left us with some guys who were quite physical but not the most talented,' Evans explains.

'Fortunately there was a good flow of good lads coming through the system at the time. We still had the experienced players like John Barnes and Ian Rush and then the younger lads to work with them.' The crop included goalkeeper David James, defender Rob Jones, midfielder Jamie Redknapp and locally born forward Steve McManaman.

That season, 1994/95, Evans deployed a 3-5-2 system as opposed to the more standard 4-4-2 used across the Premier League at the time, with his wing-backs bombing forward on either side of the pitch. Liverpool finished fourth in the league and won a trophy. Against Bolton Wanderers at Wembley in the final of the League Cup, McManaman blossomed in his free role behind the strikers as he scored two terrific dribbling-and-striding strikes in the 2-1 win.

'McManaman just had the ability to go past people and was very straightforward with it,' says Evans. 'He wasn't all step-overs. It was cut inside, head up, pace. Once he was past that back four and the defenders were running back he was making chances. He was a great asset for us.'

Also emerging alongside McManaman and the rest of that younger group was another exciting player, from the south of Liverpool, who in 1994/95 had topped the scoring charts with more than 30 goals in all competitions.

Backs to the Country

July 1981. In the Liverpool district of Toxteth, frustrations over high unemployment and poor relations between police and the community's predominantly black population had erupted into violent riots. That year, 20 per cent of people were out of work in the city, more than the double the national figure, and during those nights of violence hundreds of arrests were made as hundreds of rioters and police were injured. People from different parts of the city had joined in and buildings and cars had burned. Just as Toxteth was the stage, the longstanding frustrations of a city's population were the story.

In the aftermath of the riots, the Conservative MP Michael Heseltine was despatched to the city to walk the streets to try to understand what had gone wrong. While Margaret Thatcher's Chancellor of the Exchequer Geoffrey Howe was suggesting the 'managed decline' of troubled inner cities like Liverpool ('I fear that Merseyside is going to be much the hardest nut to crack', Howe said of the region specifically), Heseltine pressed for a path based on urban development underpinned by both public and private investment. The regeneration of the Albert Dock was one such showcase example.

The overtures of Heseltine were set against the backdrop of the activities of the city's Labour council, which included a number of hard-left Trotskyist Militant members. After winning power in 1983, they went on to set an illegal, loss-making budget for the city – effectively giving the finger to central government – and 47 of its councillors were expelled from office.

'I remember it [Toxteth] as being a safe enough place to grow up, and I didn't remember ever having much trouble as a kid,' the Liverpool star Robbie Fowler would write in his 2005 autobiography of the area he grew up in. 'There were always places you shouldn't go, and people you should avoid, but the fact is, you didn't go far at all anyway.

'[A]t one end of my road was the school, and at the other end was an all-weather football pitch, and for me, that was the extent of my world ... I don't remember much about it [the riots], because I was too young [Fowler was six at the time] ... too little to understand ... but I do know it happened right outside our front door ... on the pavement right outside my front door, about ten feet away from where I was watching the telly.'

Fowler was born in 1975 and joined Liverpool's youth set-up when he was 16. Left-footed with superb striking technique, he was a devastatingly accurate and prolific in front of goal. By 17, he had made his debut for the first team, scoring against Fulham in a League Cup tie at Craven Cottage. In the return leg at Anfield, he netted *five* times and afterwards celebrated at home with a can of Irn Bru. In his breakthrough 1993/94 season, Fowler scored 18 times.

The young striker played with enthusiasm and a smile on his face. The following season against Arsenal at

Anfield in 1994, he hit a wonderful five-minute hat-trick – three of his 31 goals that season. He was the undoubted star of Evans's emerging side, representing along with McManaman and Redknapp its fresh-faced possibilities. Fowler would be especially adored by the Liverpool fans who in time would call him 'God'.

During 1995/96, he was unstoppable again, this time with 36 goals. Against Manchester United at Old Trafford in October, when Eric Cantona returned after his kung fu kick ban, he hit two brilliant strikes. His first was a rocket at Peter Schmeichel's near post, then came a delicate lob over the Danish keeper after he had firmly knocked the United defender Gary Neville out of the way. Later on that season at Anfield, against Aston Villa, Fowler scored one of my favourite goals ever: receiving the ball far out from McManaman and with his back to goal, he flicked it past Steve Staunton, turned and took it on with a touch before triggering the sweetest bending-away strike into the left-hand side of the net.

Roy Evans loved him. 'Robbie, to be fair, is up there with the very best, with people like Ian Rush. He was Johnny-on-the-spot, always in the right position at the right time. If a loose ball came into the penalty area, he'd be there and would put it into the back of the net. That's not something you can coach. It's something that's very natural. He had a very sharp brain and would take things on board that you said to him. And he scored great goals.'

Spice Boys

For the 1995/96, season Evans made two additions to his squad. He spent £4.5m on Bolton Wanderers' Birkenhead-born Liverpool fan Jason McAteer. McAteer would be used by Evans as a right wing-back, able to push forward energetically and add to the team's attacks. Then a club and British record fee of £8.5m went on Nottingham Forest's striker Stan Collymore, a tremendously talented forward – powerful yet elegant – who on paper looked the ideal foil for Fowler.

Evans now had Fowler, Collymore or club legend Ian Rush to pick from upfront. McManaman roamed in behind in his free role. Redknapp, John Barnes or Michael Thomas competed for the two midfield spots. Rob Jones was the wing-back on the left, McAteer on the right. Phil Babb, Mark Wright, John Scales or Neil Ruddock were Evans's options for the three centre-back positions. David James stood behind them in goal.

By the end of October 1995, Liverpool sat third in the Premier League, five points behind Kevin Keegan's pace-setting Newcastle side. So far they'd despatched Tottenham (3-1), Blackburn (3-0), Bolton (5-2) and Manchester City (6-0) with exciting, free-flowing attacking play. Fowler had reached ten goals. The author and Liverpool supporter John Williams would describe Evans's emerging team as '*the* passing team in England in the mid-1990s'.

Then came what the VHS season review of that season (which on the cover featured Fowler wearing that year's excellent green-and-white four-quadrant Adidas strip) would call 'Black November' – a torrid month in which Liverpool lost three times and drew once in the league, along with exiting the League Cup at Newcastle. 'For some reason we had a really poor month' remembers Evans. 'That probably cost us the league that year. I don't know why what happened or why. Sometimes you just lose that little bit of confidence. With the class of players we had it was very difficult to pinpoint, a little spell where we couldn't score and we couldn't defend. Sometimes it's about mentality.'

Around this period there were disconcerting rumours surrounding the exploits of some of the Liverpool players, which, when added together, built up to a picture of indiscipline and casual attitudes, a lack of drive and determination and, perhaps worst of all considering the club's rich heritage, unprofessionalism. These rumours and stories would help explain that team's ultimate failings.

First there was the excessive drinking. While in the mid–90s such activities were still prevalent at many, if not most football clubs, Liverpool had their fair of alcohol-related stories at the time. There were tales of players leaving straight after home games to go out partying in London, or closer to home the big nights at Liverpool's famous Cream nightclub. As Neil Ruddock would recall, 'We had a saying, "Win, draw or lose; first to the bar for booze."'

There were stories like the players passing around a £1 coin to hold *during* matches, with whoever ended up with the coin at the end of the game buying the drinks that evening. 'There was one game when we were lining up to defend a free kick,' Ruddock would remember, 'and it [the coin] was being passed along the wall. We lost that one 2-1.'

Further to that, there were stories of punch-ups between players – Ruddock and Fowler, for example (or more specifically, Ruddock punching Fowler after a flight back from a European away tie). Or of Stan Collymore never quite fitting in with the squad – he would last only two seasons at the club before being moved on to Aston Villa. There were accusations over poor time-keeping – on one occasion Rob Jones was late for training because he had fallen asleep at some traffic lights. And in general, casual attitudes in training such as Ruddock (again) walking out on to the training pitch eating a bacon sandwich. Still to come were Jason McAteer's Wash & Go television advert and David James modelling for Armani.

In July 1996 the Spice Girls had high-kicked their way into the music charts with their single 'Wannabe'. By March 1997, for all of the fun they appeared to be having away from the football pitch, Evans's group had earned themselves the nickname, the 'Spice Boys'. It was all a bit *Loaded* magazine, lairy lads getting up to mischief. All a bit *Dumb and Dumber.*

'I thought the whole "Spice Boys" thing was unfair,' says Evans. 'They were good pros, good lads and they all had a bit of personality. They lived a life outside of football. Of course the media is always quick to jump on anything that they think isn't perfect. At that time the players were starting to stand out more, become more popular on the television, more popular than they've ever been. If you made a mistake or did something wrong, the press and the media was all over you. But I liked the fact they had a bit of personality.'

Liverpool is a working-class city, though, where its footballers are placed on pedestals. Expectations will always be high, particularly among Liverpool supporters. For a club with a heritage of such professionalism and winning, shenanigans like this did not match up with the standards of those times and of those levels. Around this time Premier League players were earning around £2,500 a week on average (a number of the league's top players by now were taking north of £10,000) and Liverpool fans were paying good money to watch their team play at Anfield. As Jamie Redknapp would recall more critically of the situation at the time, 'There were one of two things Roy [Evans] could have nipped in the bud sooner … We needed the iron fist a little bit more.'

* * * *

After 'Black November', Evans's side managed to recover and go on a 15-game unbeaten run in the league with Fowler scoring more of his beautiful goals: he scored two against Manchester United at Anfield in December – one of them a delicate free kick that totally wrong-footed Peter Schmeichel. Two more came against Aston Villa in the semi-final of the FA Cup at Old Trafford. The first was a header and the second a left-foot half-volley floated into the corner of Mark Bosnich's net. 'You are looking at a goalscoring genius,' the Sky commentator Martin Tyler said of that one.

Despite the upturn in form and the excellence of the likes of Fowler and McManaman, Liverpool still lacked the cutting edge of top teams of their past. Two games in early April highlighted their ups and downs and their inconsistency of the period. First at Anfield they hosted Keegan's Newcastle who led Liverpool by five points in the league with a game in hand over them. The encounter is one of the Premier League's classic matches where Liverpool had led twice and trailed once before eventually taking the 4-3 injury-time win. Three days later, they then lost 1-0 to relegation-threatened Coventry City at Highfield Road.

Liverpool would finish the season third in the table, their best finish for five seasons. Many believed they could have challenged harder and finished closer than the 11 points difference that ended up between them and the eventual champions Manchester United.

* * * *

There would be one last chance of glory in the 1995/96 FA Cup Final against Manchester United. Despite Liverpool's flaws, it was a contest that still promised so much, pitting two very good sides against each other for the season's finale.

Hours before kick-off, the BBC's Des Lynam greeted the TV audience on *Cup Final Grandstand* with, 'Good day to you from Wembley'. The coverage included clips of the teams at their hotel and of the supporters gathering on Wembley Way. The game itself was a poor affair, though, failing to live up to its hype. While on the day Liverpool at times looked comfortable on the ball, they weren't able to make inroads to the United goal. McManaman was largely stifled as he was harassed by Roy Keane, and thus the supply to Fowler and Ian Rush was cut. In the 86th minute, Eric Cantona struck through a crowd of Liverpool players to win the cup and take the Double to Old Trafford.

'We didn't play, they didn't play,' recalls Evans of the big day. 'Unfortunately, they got the goal and that cost us the cup. Nobody really deserved to win it, but they scored the goal which we probably should have defended better. Obviously with it being two big teams everyone thought it was going to be a great game, but it wasn't. It was a poor final.'

What the final would mostly be remembered for, though, were the cream Armani suits that the Liverpool players wore before the game. Journalist and Liverpool fan Brian Reade was unimpressed by his team's infamous choice of clothing. 'As they strolled around in their matching designer suits and shades, half of them looking like they were trying to be spotted by a modelling agency, we just looked on in shock and amazement,' he would write in his book, *43 Years With the Same Bird: A Liverpudlian Love Affair*. 'Their get-up and their body language said everything we'd feared to speak about them. It said we want different things in life from you.'

That quote again from Manchester United defender David May about the suits Liverpool players were wearing that day, 'We thought they looked like fucking knobs.'

Solidarity

While I'm in the city I meet with Tony Nelson at The Casa on Hope Street, not far up the hill in the centre of Liverpool, along from the striking Metropolitan Cathedral. Previously The Casa was an after-hours drinking establishment, the Casablanca, and before that a sea merchant's house. Today it acts as a community support and arts hub, political meeting place and bar. Nelson is a former Liverpool dockworker who is based here.

'I started on the Liverpool docks at 15 years old in 1973,' explains Nelson, sitting upstairs in a quiet office away from the bustle downstairs. 'I'm from a family of Liverpool dockers. My dad was a docker, I had seven uncles who were all dockers and five aunties who were married to dockers.

'It was all about community on the docks. It wasn't a job, it was really a way of life. You didn't just work with your colleagues, you also socialised with them. You went for a drink after work with them. There were lots and lots of pubs next to where we worked. We looked after each other and if you had any problems yourself, you were looked after. Our work wasn't easy. It was hard work, very physical, unloading and loading the containers from the ships. But that aspect of it was made easier by the solidarity with the people you worked with. You actually looked forward to going to work. It was this big family community and that's what made us strong.'

Growing up, Nelson was a big Liverpool fan. 'I've supported them all my life,' he says. 'Home games and away games – I enjoyed travelling away on the minibus. For Anfield we'd finish work at 1pm on a Saturday, walk up to the pub and have a few pints. We'd sing a few songs, then go and watch the match. I used to walk over near to Everton's ground then across to Anfield. It doesn't take long to walk through Stanley Park and round to the Kop. It was amazing on there because every game you'd manage to find the same spot to stand. You were talking almost 30,000 people stood behind the goal. All working-class. Lots of them were dockers.'

Until the late 1960s, the work and livelihoods of the 10,000 workers on the Liverpool docks had been governed by an uncertain system of casualisation where each day workers would stand outside the gates of the docks to offer their labour for the day, waiting to find out whether or not they would be selected for work. In effect, it was a zero-hours contract system for the time. In 1967, this system was abolished, bringing a new era of decasualisation: a more settled routine of shifts and working hours and no more standing at the gates.

Over the decades, this industry changed all around those men as larger-scale container shipping and technological advances removed manual elements from the job. Meanwhile shipping spread to other ports in Europe and England. By 1989, only 1,000 registered dockworkers remained in Liverpool. That same year decasualisation was effectively ended by the Thatcher government with the abolition of the long-standing National Dock Labour Scheme (which had provided various protections relating to dockworkers' jobs), its removal paving the way for a return to the old ways of casualisation. More flexible working conditions came in which made the routine of work more difficult for the dockers. Now they were effectively always on call, even on scheduled days off from work; they were working longer hours and were fatigued.

'Things had been building up over a number of years,' says Nelson. 'There were a lot of issues. A lot of people were getting disciplines. People refusing to go to work to do half an hour shifts just after they'd done another shift a few hours before, things like that. You'd say, "I'm not doing it." It was physically impossible to do. Then they'd discipline you. That's what was happening.'

In September 1995, five men working for the sub-contractor company Torside Ltd were dismissed following a dispute over an overtime shift they were asked to work. Events escalated between the company, the sacked men and their colleagues and by the following day the rest of the 80-strong workforce had been dismissed as well. The men picketed the nearby Seaforth Dock where, in solidarity with their cause, the dockers there refused to pass. These men would also be sacked along with the Torside employees and subsequently locked out from their place of work, over 300 men in total.

'The dispute was not about Torside itself,' explains Nelson. 'What happened there just lit the touch-paper. It was always going to happen somewhere. When the picket line went up, people started ringing round to let people know. I was on the twilight shift at Seaforth, 5pm I'd started that day. The news just travelled round. We didn't have mobile phones then, but everyone got to know pretty soon what was going on and that began a two-and-a-half year dispute.'

As the dockers struggled for reinstatement of their jobs, the action would become one of the country's longest ever industrial disputes.

'I was in charge of the picket lines on the docks,' says Nelson. 'You'd get up at 5am, travel and get to the picket line at about 6am. In the winter it was hard. We'd picket until about 9am, go away and come back again. We kept on doing it. We had afternoon pickets, night pickets. That carried on and on. It was physically exhausting. But it kept the men together rather than them sitting at home and festering.'

A collection of photographs of the dispute taken by Dave Sinclair, *Dockers: The '95 to '98 Liverpool Lockout*, covered the bleakness and struggle of the dispute. In those photos, people look cold yet determined, stood around in woolly hats; the docks and cranes and containers loomed behind their picket lines. In one of the photos Tony Nelson is stood there, his face concentrated, his lumberjack check shirt tucked into his jeans. It was a hard time and there was no pay for the men as they struggled on. The dispute would continue right on through the rest of 1995, all of '96, '97 and into '98.

'I stopped going to the games around that time,' says Nelson. 'I watched it on TV when I could. I was busy with the dispute. There was too much going on at the time for me. I just hated all that "Spice Boys" shite and everything.'

* * * *

Despite the various criticisms levelled at Evans's Liverpool side at times, 1996/97 would represent a great opportunity for the team to push on for Premier League success. After Euro 96, the Czech Republic midfielder Patrik Berger arrived at the club for £3.25m and Fowler would again be prolific in front of goal. In one game against Middlesbrough, he grabbed four goals and in another, the 4-3 defeat of Newcastle at Anfield (a repeat scoreline of the previous season's classic), he hit another two, including the later winner. It would be another 30-plus goal season for him. Again the team was entertaining and as the season progressed they made a strong challenge for the title, competing with Manchester United, Newcastle United (now featuring Alan Shearer) and an emerging Arsenal.

On New Year's Day 1997, Liverpool were top of the Premier League, clear of Arsenal by two points. As the months progressed, however, particularly as the season entered its closing stages, their soft centre cost them at key moments. Ground was lost when it could have been retained and built on, and the 'Spice Boys' floundered.

David James would receive particular criticism for his at times erratic goalkeeping, something that would be a storyline of most of his season: 14 dropped catches, his calamitous tally for the season as Liverpool dropped points.

In April '97, Evan's men lost 2-1 to Coventry at Anfield and later drew with Everton at Goodison Park. With four matches to go, Manchester United came to town. Liverpool sat two points behind them but had played a game more than their visitors. That day James twice flapped at crosses that led directly to two of United goals. United's 3-1 victory saw them leave Anfield five points ahead of Liverpool. 'We defended like strangers who'd just met up in the park after a 24-hour drugs bender,' wrote Brian Reade in *43 Years With the Same Bird*.

After the United defeat, Liverpool managed only one more win from their last three games, eventually finishing fourth in the table, seven points behind champions United and behind Newcastle and Arsenal on goal difference.

As Robbie Fowler would later reflect on that season, which he saw as a great opportunity missed, 'We should have won the Premiership that year. It was a strange season, and a frustrating one, because for much of it we were close to achieving something, but we were being undermined by the problems that ate away at the morale of the squad.'

Dogs of War

Just a mile from Anfield across Stanley Park sits Goodison Park, opened in 1892 and home to Everton Football Club. The old ground is hemmed in by rows of terraced houses and is oldschool to say the least – as evidenced by the wooden boards under the seats on the upper tier of the Howard Kendall Gwladys Street End stand where in late 2017 I sat for a game. On one corner of the ground is St Luke's Church and on Goodison Road the giant Main Stand lurches over the houses and the Winslow Hotel. The last major development at Goodison came in 1994 with the construction of the Park End Stand. Standing around the ground feels a little like being stuck in a time warp, albeit a good one – you can feel its history and soul.

During the 1970s and early 1980s, Everton had languished in the shadow of their more successful red neighbours before emerging in the mid-80s as their big rivals in the First Division. Manager Howard Kendall built a championship-winning side in 1984/85 and 1986/87 and they lifted the FA Cup in '84, then the European Cup Winners' Cup in '85. Between them, Everton and Liverpool made the city the footballing capital of the country when the First Division title remained on Merseyside for seven years from 1982.

As many would observe of life in the city, at a time of such high unemployment – 27 per cent by 1985 – footballing success at least kept up some kind of morale.

Had it not been for the post-Heysel ban on English clubs from Europe, Everton would have qualified for European competition in four of its five seasons. For them, the ban froze their success and stunted their momentum, before leading to their decline. They lost star striker Gary Lineker to Barcelona, Kendall to Athletic Bilbao, then Gary Stevens and Trevor Steven to Glasgow Rangers. As would be the case for their city neighbours, for Everton the 1990s would prove a decade of difficult adjustment, certainly when compared to the heights of the previous ten years.

* * * *

Back in 1986, Dave Watson joined Everton from Norwich City and would go on to make over 400 appearances in the blue shirt. The tough-tackling centre-back made his last appearance for the club in 2000 and, speaking down the phone one spring afternoon, he remembers his time on Merseyside fondly.

'The team had started to break up a little once the ban from Europe started,' says Watson. 'To be honest I didn't think we would slide as far as we did. We got into some really tricky positions, fighting relegation a few times and what have you, but back when I joined, I never would have imagined that kind of scenario would be coming up for us.'

Everton spent much of the first two seasons of the Premier League in its lower reaches. In 1993/94, they battled to avoid relegation to the second tier, finishing the campaign with a last-day and late 3-2 win over Wimbledon at Goodison. They had trailed 2-0, but managed to rally and ensure their survival by two points.

'Obviously that was a very tough season,' says Watson. 'Mike Walker had taken charge of the club and I think he found it difficult. Mike had been at Norwich and done well, but he'd got a few big characters with us who he struggled to handle. I don't think he handled them as well as he could and we weren't quite good enough on the pitch. Things went to the last game of the season with Wimbledon. We were getting beat 2-0, but gave a tremendous fightback to win and stay up.

'The feeling after that game was such relief. Everton had mostly always been in the top flight [the last time they had been in the Second Division had been in 1953/54] and as captain of the football club it had been a big weight on my shoulders, you know. Was I going to be the only captain to get Everton relegated? So to win and stay up was a massive relief.'

The following year when Everton struggled again, Walker was sacked. Joe Royle, once a player with the club during the 60s and 70s, arrived from Oldham to replace him. Such was his popularity both in the stands with the fans and in the dressing room with his players, he would prove a hugely positive influence. Royle galvanised the team and kept them up that season, albeit in less dramatic fashion than the year before – safety being assured at Ipswich with one game of 1994/95 to spare.

'I'd played with Joe when I was at Norwich,' recalls Watson. 'He'd come in and had been great for us. It was a difficult season and he knew exactly what the lads wanted – a bit of humour around the place and a bit of fun. He had a massive presence and helped take a lot of pressure off the players. He showed how just talking to people and coming in with a smile on his face could help. When he took over at Everton, it was just the same [he was] a big presence with lots of humour. The lads had a smile on their faces again and wanted to play for him. When he walked in the room you knew he was the man for the job.

'Joe was fairly straightforward in his approach to games. Play off the front man, get the ball forward quick and pressure teams all over the pitch. We were full of energy and had some real tough characters like Joe Parkinson, Barry Horne and John Ebbrell in midfield. They won lots of battles for us. We showed commitment and that's what the fans wanted to see from an Everton team. If they didn't see the work ethic, you'd lose them. With Joe, we had that.'

That season, those midfielders in particular helped earn Everton the nickname the 'Dogs of War'. 'That sounded great,' says Watson. 'It was definitely the kind of approach we needed at the time.'

During 1994/95, a happier distraction for Royle's Everton had been the FA Cup as round by round they built up a positive and distracting run against Derby County, Bristol City, Norwich City and Newcastle United. For the semi-final it was Tottenham Hotspur at Elland Road, Leeds. Everton won 4-1 as Matt Jackson, Graham Stuart and Daniel Amokachi (twice) got the goals to send them through to Wembley to face Manchester United.

'The cup run really helped us,' believes Watson. 'It really took the pressure off trying to win the matches in the league and it gave the fans something to cheer about. Tottenham had star players like Jurgen Klinsmann and Teddy Sheringham and everyone fancied them for that semi-final. But we beat them well.'

* * * *

Dave Kelly was just eight years old when he went to his first Everton game in 1966, the year that the Merseysiders won the FA Cup and England the World Cup (Goodison Park had been one of the venues for the tournament). Along with his season ticket at Goodison for the Park End stand behind the goal, Kelly owns a single prized share in his football club. He sports a grey beard and his glasses are perched on his head as if ready to be lowered should they be needed. For years and years he has followed Everton home and away.

'In 1994, we had played Leeds United away at Elland Road,' he remembers. 'That was the week before the Wimbledon survival game and we'd been turned over 3-0. Losing to Leeds had put us into the relegation places, so we were left with that home game against Wimbledon. I can remember walking away from Elland Road that day and getting back on the minibus. There was a big argument on the way back about how we were doomed, that we'd gone. At the time it felt like the club was in terminal decline. We were slumbering.

'One thing I will say is, even though we'd had all of the cup finals and everything in the 80s, which had been great,

148

that Wimbledon game in '94 is probably my favourite as a fan. It's a strange thing to say, but I got more satisfaction from that one, I think. Well, more relief than satisfaction.'

The season after the Wimbledon great escape, Kelly was back in Leeds for the FA Cup semi-final against Tottenham.

'I'll always remember that one,' says Kelly, 'because of how Elland Road is laid out, with one big stand for one side of the pitch, our fans had all three of the other smaller sides. We were behind both goals and down one side of the pitch, so it made it seem like it was full of Evertonians.'

The weekend before the 1995 FA Cup Final, Manchester United had narrowly lost out to Blackburn Rovers in the Premier League title race, but Everton still travelled to Wembley to face them as firm underdogs. Nevertheless, the fans and all those associated with the club couldn't wait for the big day.

'Driving to Wembley it just seemed to be all blue and white,' recalls Dave Watson. 'There were Evertonians everywhere. It had been a while since we'd won a trophy – I think it had been the league in '87 – so for us it was a big occasion. I was 33, so there weren't many more chances left for me to play in an FA Cup Final. I didn't want to let the moment pass and wanted to make sure the rest of the team didn't either.'

The final turned out to be a dull affair, certainly for the neutral. The midfield tussle between Joe Parkinson and Barry Horne and United's Paul Ince and Roy Keane was intriguing – as was Watson's and Mark Hughes's – but that was about it.

Everton's goal came after half an hour. Swedish winger Anders Limpar picked up the ball from his own half and dashed forward, feeding Matt Jackson on the right. His pass found Graham Stuart who hit the bar with his strike before the ball bounced out for striker Paul Rideout. Rideout beat Denis Irwin in the air and headed past Peter Schmeichel for 1-0.

The minutes ticked by, veteran goalkeeper Neville Southall made a few vital saves to keep United out and Everton held on for the unexpected win. The FA Cup was Watson's to lift.

'The final whistle was the best sound that day,' Watson says. 'It was just magnificent. Looking around at your team-mates and the happiness on their faces, knowing how as a team we'd done it together, it was just great to see. Everyone was celebrating together, the players and the supporters.

'Me and the wife actually had the cup in our bedroom that night. We had all the family staying in the hotel, so the next morning they all came to the room and everyone got a hold of the FA Cup.

'On the way home to Liverpool, the coach actually stopped off at a McDonald's, so we could all get some food. From all of the glory and the glitz, then we were in McDonald's getting a burger ... Well, it's a tough old life isn't it, mate?

'Wembley was an incredible day out,' recalls Dave Kelly. 'It was a day filled with anticipation, then joy, then the plans for the great things that lay ahead. It felt like we had turned a corner. It felt like we were going in the right direction.'

Premier League survival. Wembley. McDonald's. For fans like Kelly, this was the beginning of Everton's 1990s recovery, the moment just before their return and rise.

The following season they paid Manchester United £5m for their Russian winger Andrei Kanchelskis and finished sixth in the Premier League. In 1996/97, they spent £3.5m on Gary Speed from Leeds United and £5.75m on Nick Barmby from Middlesbrough, though this time they slumped to 15th. By that point Royle had left and in 1997/98 Howard Kendall took over for another spell. He lasted just one season before Walter Smith took his place for what would be another year of treading water. Twenty-plus seasons on and Everton remain a top-flight club. There have been no more trophies, though, since the FA Cup in '95.

* * * *

Today Dave Kelly is involved with Fans Supporting Foodbanks, an alliance of Everton and Liverpool supporters that since 2015 has collected food before both clubs' home games. As the group's motto goes, 'It's not charity, it's solidarity', and according to Kelly 25 per cent of the food donated to the North Liverpool Foodbank is distributed outside Anfield and Goodison before their matches.

Kelly is a true Scouser, not a Liverpudlian, as he points out to me. To clarify, 'Liverpool fans are Liverpudlians. Everton fans are Evertonians. People from Liverpool are Scousers.' And Kelly, the Evertonian and Scouser, cares deeply about his city and its people.

'I was a construction worker and I can remember when Thatcher first got elected [in 1979]. I remember being at work the following day and there being a discussion about how the world was going to change, and not particularly for the better.' Within a couple of years there were riots in many of England's major cities, including Liverpool.

Both Anfield and Goodison Park sit in the constituency of Walton where alongside the wealth of its two Premier

League football clubs there are some of the poorest neighbourhoods in the land. 'In times of adversity people in this city will always stand together,' explains Kelly. 'People who are victims of austerity and the Universal Credit system need support. There is a humanitarian crisis in our city. Not just in our city but in every major town and city in the country. So to me this is working-class solidarity. It's us doing what we've always done, looking after our own.

'Liverpool has got a long and proud track record of standing together, particularly in times of adversity. We stand together as one. In the 80s I used to have a little Ford Escort van that I used to put the loud hailer on the roof and drive round Kirkby where I live. We supported the miners' strike [1984–85] and we'd go driving round the streets with it on saying, "Don't let Thatcher starve the miners back to work" and collect food for them. Fast-forward to the dockers' and it was the same thing for them. I collected food and stood on the picket line with them.'

* * * *

Midway through 1997, the Liverpool dockers' dispute was more than two years in. The hundreds of sacked and locked-out workers were still out on the picket lines and still there was some way to go in their struggle. Times were hard.

Back in the upstairs room of The Casa on Hope Street with Tony Nelson, he recounts how the dispute was taking its toll on his colleagues and friends. 'It was a long, long time and people were just getting exhausted,' he says. 'Some people disagreed with carrying on and some people just couldn't. Because I was in charge of organising the picketing I could see was the numbers out there going down. Not because they'd had enough, they just couldn't carry on. Two-and-a-half years on the picket line, it was exhausting, physically and mentally.'

On the ground, support had come from some of the Liverpool footballers. Norwegian left-back Stig Inge Bjornebye would stop by. 'He came down on his own,' recalls Nelson. 'Lovely man. What I really liked about him was that he didn't announce himself. He just drove down and stood at the end on his own. He wouldn't talk to anyone, just stood there. He did it a few times. He was quiet but was there to support us.'

In March '97, after his goal during a European Cup Winners' Cup quarter-final home tie against Norwegian side SK Brann, Robbie Fowler lifted his red Liverpool top to reveal a t-shirt supporting the dockers' fight. This brought the campaign national media attention and Fowler a £900 fine from UEFA. 'I got a stern warning and fined about a grand, which was a disgrace when you think about how justified the cause was,' Fowler would recall of the incident. Apparently the t-shirt idea had been Steve McManaman's. 'Lots of my dad's mates are dockworkers,' he said. 'It wasn't a case of coming out and supporting them because it was the correct thing to do; I simply knew them, I used to have the occasional drink with them. I knew the predicament they were in and I wanted to give them support as friends.' Downstairs in The Casa on the wall in the bar is a photo of Fowler in that t-shirt. Not every 1990s footballer wearing a red Liverpool shirt was a Spice Boy.

'You use every kind of publicity you can,' explains Nelson. 'We needed as much as we could get and things like that got us good press and that was great. It meant a lot and things like that kept us going. The whole thing about being on strike is that you are isolated. You are starved, not just of food or money, but of a voice. It helped us a lot. We were a long time in. We were getting tired. Money was tight. Some of us had been arrested – I think we'd had over a hundred arrests. I was arrested a few times myself, locked up for obstruction. Then I went back down to the picket line. When Robbie was in the papers and we were on the picket line, he was fined £900. We got in touch and offered to pay it, but he said, "No, I'll pay it."'

In 1996 the filmmaker Ken Loach had come to Liverpool to make a documentary about the dispute. *The Flickering Flame* covered the mass meetings and passionate speeches and featured shots of the men stood outside the gates of the docks. Panning shots show the vastness of its landscape. In the documentary people share their experiences and struggles. 'There are people who will lose their homes if the dispute continues,' says one. 'People are starving,' says another.

Extra Time

In Liverpool I also meet the author, Liverpool fan and former manager of the band The Farm, Kevin Sampson. A season ticket holder at Anfield since the 1970s, Sampson buys me a cup of tea in a quiet café in the city centre on Tithebarn Street and immediately makes me feel welcome (in a text after we meet up he calls me 'la', which I think means 'mate' in Liverpool).

'Here's a potted history of me at Anfield. My dad used to take me to the games on the Kemlyn Road Stand. That was the late 60s. I spent a lot of the time looking left towards the Kop and I was mesmerised, not just by the noise but also the spectacle – all the swaying people on there.

'Dad died in September '76, so me and my brother inherited his season ticket. We used to alternate who would use it and the one who didn't have it for that particular game would go on the Kop. We each used to have our own spec on there ['spec' means the place where you would stand or sit in the ground – only in Liverpool have I heard people say this]. I went high up. If you were looking at the Kop, two-thirds up to the left, that was it. A fantastic spec. When they built the Centenary Stand above the Kemyln Road Stand [another tier of seats in 1992], I was on the fourth row, very close to the halfway line. I'm in the Main Stand now opposite.

'By the season you're asking me about [1996/97] Liverpool had drifted. It had been quite a few years since we'd won the league, but for a lot of us the penny hadn't quite dropped in terms of how drastic that demise had been, or would continue to be. Never would it have entered my head that it would be so many years without us winning the league again. As a fan my thinking and mentality was; If we don't win it this year we're bound to be back up there next year, or the year after. Time goes by and suddenly it's five years, ten years, since you've won a league. That's how it had become at Liverpool.

'I still thought we had a really great nucleus of young players though and that once they'd gelled they would be something else. But at the same time you were going to the games and seeing your team getting turned over by Coventry and Wimbledon. By that point the penny had started to drop. We were getting left behind, we were off the pace. I don't think that people at the club anywhere properly acknowledged our malaise.

'We had Robbie of course and he meant everything. With Robbie it was pure adoration. I'm not sure if it was the fans or Steve McManaman that gave him the nickname "God", but that was how we looked upon him. He was so much a representation of what we were all about as fans. You could identify with him. He wasn't just a local lad. When he spoke in interviews, he sounded like someone who was no different to us.

'He was so unconventional-looking as well, the opposite of an athlete, but he had everything. One thing that struck me early on was his technique, the lack of back-lift in his shots. He seemed to get enormous power into them and incredible accuracy. His left foot was laser-guided. I think whoever you are or whoever you support there's nothing better than seeing one of your own come through the ranks, especially if they're as good as he was. Robbie produced for us right from the start.

'In terms of the "Spice Boys" team, I think they were rightly derided. Liverpool, for all of its geography, is a large area but a small city. People knew everything, when the players had been out in nightclubs and that kind of thing. There were so many stories about things that had happened in training, who'd been parking in whose parking spots [namely, Roy Evans's] and smirking when they were pulled up for it, pretending they didn't know what they were doing. It was totally puerile and counter-productive. There seemed to be no respect for the leadership and that went all the way down to the performances in the games.

'The way I see it, all too often those players were willing to settle for less when winning was within their grasp. It didn't seem to hurt them enough when they got beat. At times it was almost as if the weight of expectation to win was so much that it was almost easier to throw in the towel.

'Now for those cup final suits [in 1996]. Just to balance that a little bit. I thought they were brilliant. They were Armani, nice ties. If we'd have ended up winning the cup, people might have looked at them as symbolic of the good times coming back. Instead they became so embedded with an anti-climactic end to the season and what was a miserable day at Wembley. But I definitely thought they were more than capable of beating that Man United. United got one of the scruffiest goals ever and won the cup with it. So the suits were not my problem. It was more, you know, what was going on with the general attitude of the team and the club at the time.

'It sounds weird to be calling someone out as being too nice. It's not a normal thing you'd say – that to have a kind character is a negative thing. But with Roy Evans, in the world of the football manager, you probably do need to be more ruthless. I think he deserves a lot of credit as a forward-thinking strategist. The system he played with the wing-backs, for example, was exciting. He was a football man. But for me he just wasn't a leader to instil that sort of discipline and respect in the team.'

* * * *

For the 1997/98 campaign Sampson charted his travels following Liverpool all season in his book, *Extra Time: A Season in the Life of a Football Fan*. In it he writes about adjusting to Liverpool's increasingly non-dominant position in English football. 'Quite simply,' he begins, 'we need to win the league again,' before going on to detail the fun he has with mates going to away games and the like, all of the excitement and frustrations of being a Liverpool fan in the 1990s: arriving ten minutes before kick-off at Newcastle having travelled via the Lake District, across from Carlisle, only for his friend to realise he'd left his ticket back in Merseyside. Or getting the 8.45am train to go down to London for Wimbledon away on the first game of the season – 'It's pathetic how excited we are.' Then in more anxious and perhaps profound moments, noting how 'everything is under constant scrutiny and questioning of the fans. Everything from the players' wage packets to their social habits to their motives and motivation. The fans are paranoid … We're panicking. Nobody really knows what's up, how it happened or how to get things back to normal, but we are flapping.'

For Robbie Fowler, 1997/98 would be a frustrating time of injury setbacks that would cause him to be absent for much of the season. The first came during pre-season and caused him to miss Liverpool's opening league games, followed by a season-ending knee injury at Anfield against Everton in February '98. As he would recall, 'My left knee exploded. The medial ligament was snapped, the cruciate ligament ruptured and the cartilage was torn … my knee was fucked.' Fowler would make just 28 appearances that season, scoring 13 goals. Sadly, he would never be quite the same player again.

'By that point Evans had weeded out most of the weaklings from the squad,' explains Sampson of 1997/98. Stan Collymore, for example, was an expensive departure from Anfield that summer, signing for Aston Villa for £7m. 'Evans brought in a bit of experience. The basic nucleus of the team had another year's experience of playing together. Paul Ince was yet another "final piece of the jigsaw" [the former Manchester United man having returned from Italy and Inter Milan] and Michael Owen gave us some more confidence.'

Owen was the fresh-faced, wonder-kid striker with fantastic pace who had burst into the Liverpool side at the end of the previous season with a debut goal at Wimbledon. He was only 17 and would go on to score over 100 times for Liverpool, plugging a big Fowler-shaped gap in the scoring charts. A new red star had been born but, despite this, 1997/98 was not turning out that well for them.

'It was obvious fairly early on that it wasn't happening,' recalls Sampson. 'We were schizophrenic. We would get what was considered a good win against Tottenham, then lose to Barnsley. Then lose to Southampton, Aston Villa. Even back then you couldn't really lose more than about four games a season if you were going to win the league. We'd lost about five by the end of the year. There were issues. At times that season the team would flutter their eyelids, flash a bit of leg and go on a decent run, but then go and lose to someone else.'

Evans's Liverpool came third in the Premier League. Even back in the days when a third-place finish didn't bring a place in the Champions League, it still wouldn't have been a bad result for most clubs (Liverpool would still compete in the UEFA Cup the following year). But this was Liverpool, the winning club, and eight years and counting since their last title win, Evans's men weren't getting much closer now.

In *Extra Time*, Sampson references some of the 'Spice Boys' issues, including the team's Christmas party in 1997. It took place on a Sunday night, but for some of the players continued until Monday afternoon. 'Our team has been rumoured to have a committed drinking core for some years,' Sampson wrote. 'You try to ignore it … [But] It doesn't seem right that they think so little of the hope and faith that's invested in them.'

'I'd love to hear an honest reflection of what it was like for them,' Sampson says today. 'What it was like to be part of a team that was so gifted and so brimming full of potential but which fell short so often through those seasons. It didn't seem to hurt them as much as it should have done. As a fan it hurts when you travel to the games. I know how I feel when I've been to a match and we haven't performed. But did they care as much as you cared?'

Robbie Fowler would provide one such honest assessment of his team during those mid-1990s seasons. 'Don't get me wrong, things happened and they shouldn't have,' he reflected in his autobiography. 'I look back now and I can see how close we were to becoming a truly great side. The fact that it didn't happen is a real regret … [But] if more of the players had reached the level I was at for those seasons [30-plus goals for three seasons between 1994/95 and 1996/97], then we would have won more.'

Neil Ruddock, who joined West Ham in the summer of '98, would have his own reflections, referencing in particular 1996/97 when Liverpool had run Manchester United close in the title race only to fall away at the last, 'We didn't want to be remembered as also-rans or under-achievers; but we had to accept such accusations because, from being in a strong position in the league, we let our standards slip at crucial moments. The best sides, the successful sides, don't do that.'

* * * *

The 1998/99 season brought big changes for Liverpool when Gerard Houllier was brought in to co-manage the team with Evans. Houllier knew the club from his year spent teaching in the city in the late 1970s – he'd been to Anfield and stood on the Kop for a game – and had managed Paris Saint-Germain and the French national team. He had the pedigree. Unsurprisingly, the reality of the Houllier-Evans co-manager scenario became a story of awkward semi-authority over the players and a total lack of cohesion.

Ultimately, Evans would be pushed aside and forced out. It happened after the 3-1 League Cup exit to Tottenham Hotspur in November 1998. In the Premier League, Liverpool had sat 11th in the table, having lost 2-1 at home to Derby County the previous Saturday. Following the cup defeat Evans resigned from his post: the man who had served loyally in various roles since 1965 made way to leave Houllier in sole charge.

Looking back, questions of what might have been in those last few seasons, particularly 1996/97, still linger for him. 'That season, at the latter stages, we just lost one or two games that were very costly in terms of winning the league,' he says back in his living room. 'I would say that that's the most disappointing part of my time as manager. We put ourselves in the right position but failed to capitalise on it. We made a few mistakes and just couldn't finish it off. But Manchester United were the dominant team at the time.

'In the end, I walked away because of the Gerard situation. I probably should have been stronger when it was first suggested us being co-managers. I should have stood up for myself, two managers doing the same job just didn't make sense. I should have said he could be director of football and I would stay as manager. What happened with the day-to-day running of the club was that you were making one decision and the other guy was making a different one. It started to get through to the players.

'We'd talk to each other obviously and we tried to make it work. He had some different ideas about the way we would play. It was like two fans talking together – you might both have completely different thoughts about who is your favourite player, who are the best players. It became awkward. It must have been just as difficult for him as well. Within four or five months I knew it was never going to work. So I decided to walk.'

Finishing our talk, Evans reflects finally on his character, as it was perceived by others. 'I was often nicknamed "Mr Nice Guy,"' he says, 'and I think it's nice to be called that. I could rant and rave when the players hadn't performed. I was quite capable of doing that. But if you want to call me that, I don't mind that. I can live with that.'

With sole charge of the team, Houllier would lead Liverpool to seventh in the league in 1998/99. Things were changing. That season Houllier would give a young Steven Gerrard his debut. Michael Owen would notch 23 times. Steve McManaman, out of contract in the summer of 1999, would join Real Madrid and then win the Champions League twice.

As the years rolled by, Liverpool's last league title triumph in 1989/1990 remained fixed in an ever more distant past. The club had a continental manager and perhaps their new way would help them catch up with their peers and rivals, particularly over in Manchester at

Old Trafford with United's ever-expanding trophy cabinet. In 1999, investment for the club would come from media company Granada (£22m to purchase just under ten per cent of the club). An FA Cup, League Cup and UEFA Cup treble would come in 2001.

In 2005, Houllier was replaced by the Spaniard Rafael Benitez who would deliver a famous Champions League comeback triumph against AC Milan in Istanbul. Turbulent years with American owners George Gillett and Tom Hicks would follow, before the more stable guidance of the Fenway Sports Group – a stewardship turbo-charged by the reign of Jurgen Klopp, a Shankly-esque, tracksuit-wearing, man-of-the-people manager.

* * * *

In early 1998 the Liverpool dockers' dispute reached its end, two-and-a-half years after it had begun. All of the struggle and all of the days on the picket lines were over. The redundancy offers were accepted and the jobs were mostly gone.

'We had to end the dispute unfortunately,' says Tony Nelson finally. 'It had been such a long time. We came to a deal with the company and we were made redundant. We ended it. People were exhausted. Two-and-a-half years of doing that, at the picket line every day. At the end it was a terrible, terrible day.

'My wife died right after the dispute. She passed away from cancer within four months of it ending. It was a horrific time for me. I'd lost my house, I lost my wife, lost everything. Going down to the picket line had been absolutely exhausting. The whole thing had been.'

Facing the World

Another trip over to the city on the river. Out of Sheffield, again, past Manchester and along.

At Anfield, where houses have made way for regeneration, the ground dominates. All Premier League, it's a major attraction for the city. Each year the club generates hundreds of millions of pounds for the city's economy as pilgrims to Anfield journey here from across the country and the world, spending money in the bars and restaurants and hotels.

Since the late 1990s Liverpool has welcomed increased investment to the city – from private and public, domestic and European sources – for the development of its infrastructure. This means regeneration for retail spaces, the universities, city-centre living and the continuing transformation of the waterfront. The arena at the King's Dock and the open-air retail complex Liverpool One are beacons of progress. In 1991 in the city, more than 21 per cent of people were unemployed here compared to nearly 9 per cent nationally. By 2001 this had reduced to around 10 per cent (though nationally the figure had fallen to 5 per cent). In 2008 Liverpool was announced as the European Capital of Culture. From its challenging past, here is a story of a city's gradual re-emergence.

At Anfield I nip over to the nearby petrol station to pick up a copy of the *Liverpool Echo*. Inside are pages and pages of football coverage. Naturally, Liverpool feature heavily. The 2019/20 marks 30 years since their last league title success and, before the COVID-19 lockdown put things on ice, Jurgen Klopp's men had been romping away in the table. Eventually, the season will resume and the long-awaited title will be secured.

A couple of minutes away and the red of Anfield turns to the blue of Everton and Goodison Park. Here, the brick turnstiles of the ground are built right out on to the street. While Anfield dominates, Goodison blends into its surroundings and as things stand today Evertonians live in the shadows of their neighbours. The planned new stadium at Bramley-Moore Dock may one day help revive the successes of the past.

Driving away, I join the old Dock Road from Sandhills Lane. The dock wall, or the segment of it that remains here, is in front of me and over the wall are the ruined or remaining working docks. I take a right turn and drive farther along for a quarter of an hour or so. I pass the Port of Liverpool then make it back to the beach at Crosby. The wind is blowing over the dunes and Antony Gormley's 100 cast-iron lads are still there, lining the beach and stood firm, facing the water. Their backs to the country, facing the world.

7

Revolution

Allez Les Bleus

In the summer of 1998, FIFA brought the World Cup back to Europe as, for four weeks, the world's best players from 32 nations (up from the 24 at USA 94) competed during June and July in France. As had been the case in America four years previously, the tournament would be a carnival of colour and drama. For the opening game, holders Brazil took on Scotland at the brand new, futuristic and elegant 80,000-capacity Stade de France in Paris. For their pre-match walk on the pitch the Scotland manager Craig Brown and his coaching staff wore kilts before Brazil, featuring their twice World Player of the Year striker Ronaldo, saw them off with a 2-1 victory.

The official documentary of the tournament, *La Coupe de la Gloire*, was narrated by the English actor Sean Bean, also known as Richard Sharpe in the Napoleonic Wars drama series *Sharpe* and footballer Jimmy Muir in the forgettable 1996 movie *When Saturday Comes*. 'The 16th FIFA World Cup will be the biggest festival of sport the planet has ever seen,' Bean announces to open the film.

England would be there for their first non-domestic international tournament since Sweden in 1992. The 30-mile-long Channel Tunnel had opened in 1994 and Eurostar trains took some of the thousands of England fans over to France for the games. Glenn Hoddle was in charge, having taken over from Terry Venables after Euro 96, with qualification secured after a gladiatorial 0-0 draw in Rome against Italy the previous October.

Down in the south of France, in Marseille, at the Stade Velodrome ground where earlier in the decade Chris Waddle had dazzled for Olympique, England took on Tunisia for their first game. A solid 2-0 performance saw Alan Shearer heading in the first before Manchester United's Paul Scholes hit a terrific, curling, long-range second late on. The win would be overshadowed by English thugs who, full of beer and sun, clashed with police and local French-Tunisian youths at Marseille's Old Port and Prado Beach. The trouble was a reminder that certain problems from 'Old' football still remained. Journalist Brian Glanville reported of the English hooligans who 'disgraced themselves yet again in Marseille ... the hooligan "minority" proving as hard to deter or restrain'.

England lost their next match, 2-1 to Romania in Toulouse, but managed to advance past the group stage after beating Colombia 2-0 in Lens. Argentina awaited in the second round in Saint-Etienne where Manchester United's David Beckham's silly kick-out at Diego Simeone had put England down to ten men with the game at 2-2. 'Oh no,' said ITV's Brian Moore on the commentary following Beckham's red card. Earlier in the game Liverpool's Michael Owen had made it 2-1 with a superb goal, moving at speed past two Argentine defenders before striking the ball past Carlos Roa and into the corner of his goal. Argentina equalised, then came extra time, penalties and another exit for England on the international stage (their tally of major tournament shoot-out exits now standing at three in a row). Beckham's subsequent vilification by the English press for his act of youthful petulance was extreme to say the least, and within a year of the tournament Hoddle would be out of a job, his comments linking karma and reincarnation with disability proving too unacceptable to spare him.

In the next round, Argentina were eliminated by the Netherlands, or more specifically by a sublime last-minute strike from Dennis Bergkamp: a long ball from Frank de Boer from inside his own half found the forward who, bringing it down perfectly with his right foot, took a touch to bring it inside, took out the defender Roberto Ayala before finishing with the outside of the same foot. Glanville would describe the goal as 'a small miracle of virtuosity'.

Meanwhile, the USA had lost 2-1 to Iran, a game charged with political subtext following the 1980–88 Iran-Iraq War (America having backed the latter). Morocco had drawn with Norway, then beaten Scotland and lost to Brazil to narrowly miss out on qualification to the next round. '[T]heir football charmed the world,' Bean would say of the Moroccans in *La Coupe de la Gloire*. One excellent game came in Bordeaux where Chile took on Italy. Chile's long-haired striker Marcelo Salas, about to join Lazio from Argentina's River Plate, scored twice. But Italy had Roberto Baggio and he first set up a goal before winning and converting a penalty – a moment that to some extent helped to exorcise his miss in Pasadena in the World Cup Final four years before.

The BBC's coverage from their live studio had the grand Parisian skyline as the backdrop for their pundits, a group that included Martin O'Neill. O'Neill, whose industrious Leicester City side had been brilliantly punching above their weight in the Premier League since 1996/97, was in great form – insightful and entertaining throughout.

In France, following on from their Euro 96 performances, Croatia were again excellent, knocking out Germany with a 3-0 victory at the quarter-final stage. Robert Jarni, Goran Vlaovic and their hero of Euro 96, Davor Suker, got the goals as they avenged their defeat to Germany at the same stage in England two years earlier. 'You have to go outside and die today for the Croatian flag and all the people who have given their lives,' coach Miroslav Blazevic had told his players before the Germany game, referencing the bloody Yugoslav Wars. Their World Cup would end in semi-final defeat to the hosts.

The French themselves had their maestro Zinedine Zidane, Juventus's humble and selfless creator from the tough La Castellane suburb of Marseille. The son of Algerian immigrants, Zidane had honed his footwork and skills on the concrete pitches scattered among the tower blocks of the estate where he had grown up. The extent of his intensity and abilities as a player can be seen in the documentary *Zidane: A 21ˢᵗ Century Portrait*, for which 17 cameras were trained on him for a full match in 2005 as he played in the white of Real Madrid (he would move to Madrid in 2001 for a world-record £46m fee). The footage gives a unique insight into his prowess as a player, his precision play and almost-unemotional face, dark eyes and furrowed brow. In 1998, he was France's most talented player and would be playing on home soil. In Marseille, a billboard of him overlooked the Mediterranean. 'Made in Marseille' it read (in English).

The French squad that year – 'Les Bleus' – was a truly multicultural group. Alongside goalkeeper Fabien Barthez, captain and defender Laurent Blanc, and midfielders Emmanuel Petit and Didier Deschamps, were the defenders Marcel Desailly and Lilian Thuram (respectively born in Ghana and Guadeloupe in the French West Indies), midfielder Christian Karembeu (born in New Caledonia, the Pacific Islands French territory) and Patrick Vieira (Senegal). Left-back Bixente Lizarazu was of Basque heritage and Zidane of Algerian. Forward Youri Djorkaeff and midfielder Alain Boghossian were of Armenian descent.

The group's make-up was particularly significant and powerful when considered against the views of the far-right National Front leader Jean-Marie Le Pen. Around the time Le Pen had labelled the French team 'artificial' due to its multi-ethnic make-up, referencing the players whose origins were from the former French colonies. 'When I heard Le Pen's words, it doubled my desire to win the cup for France,' Thuram would later say.

France made it all the way through to the final, beating Croatia in the last four to set-up the final with Brazil in Paris. Before the showpiece kicked off, the crowd in the Stade de France chanted 'Allez les Blues' again and again and loud.

The main drama beforehand had centred on Brazil's Ronaldo (scorer of four goals so far in the tournament). After suffering a seizure earlier in the day in his hotel room and being taken to hospital, at first he was absent from Brazil's team sheet before being riskily re-included at the last moment. In the game he would be a ghost of his brilliant self.

By half-time in the final France were 2-0 ahead – two headers from Zidane, both from corners, putting them almost out of sight. It would finish 3-0 and France were champions of the world. Afterwards Zidane's face was projected on to the Arc de Triomphe and over a million people celebrated on the Champs-Elysees. Not since the city's liberation in 1944 had there been such scenes or so many people gathered together in the capital.

The third goal that evening had come late on in the game as substitute Patrick Vieira fed fellow midfielder Emmanuel Petit to finish past Claudio Taffarel in the Brazilian goal. Petit and Vieira played their football in the Premier League, for Arsenal, and the day after their victory the *Daily Mirror* would run the headline 'ARSENAL WIN THE WORLD CUP'.

Wenger-lution

January 2018. Next up on the 1990s journey, London again. Two hours down on the Midland Main Line to St Pancras and its vast canopy, which provides a brief sanctuary from the bedlam of the capital. I take the Piccadilly line a few stops north to Arsenal, the station renamed in 1932 at the suggestion of that football club's innovative manager, Herbert Chapman. Before moving to the Gunners in the 1920s, Chapman had won three First Division titles for Huddersfield Town. Here at the tube stop the old tiles on the wall still spell out the station's previous name, Gillespie Road.

Walking out at street level, the smells of the matchday burger vans waft down the tunnel. Outside are the neat houses of N5 and along to the left are the souvenir stalls. I buy a Dennis Bergkamp badge for £3. A few ticket touts are stood around.

Turning right and on to Avenell Road there is the old East Stand of Highbury, part of what survives of Arsenal's former 38,000-capacity home. With its white-painted Art-Deco façade and red windows, the grand remains of the stand sit tight with the houses. When it opened in 1936, the East Stand was proclaimed by the club as 'a building of wonder unparalleled in football'. Today it is Grade II listed and has been converted into £1m-plus apartments. Its famous 'Marble Halls' are retained as part of a grand entrance that still features the Arsenal gun logo mosaic on the floor and a bust of Chapman (who died in 1934 after winning two First Division titles for the club). Before Arsenal matches, the team bus used to park outside the entrance and the players would walk past the fans and into the ground. Highbury was close to, and part of, its community.

Since 1991, the population of the capital has increased from around seven million to nine million people today, making it one of the world's leading multi-cultural cities. Near to Highbury there is two-mile-long Holloway Road where people from many different nations live and mix. There are flats and markets, shops and cafes, restaurants and salons. Red London buses pass up and down.

Up here, north of St Pancras, are the London boroughs of Islington and Camden, side by side, with a combined population of over half a million. Besides being home to Arsenal's Highbury stadium, during the 1990s Islington had Tony Blair as a resident (at least that is until '97 when he moved to Downing Street to implement his 'Third-Way' centre-left pro-Europe New Labour vision), and it had the fictional record shop in the Arsenal fan Nick Hornby's 1995 novel, *High Fidelity*. As would be the case across the capital during that decade, as the city moved towards it status of mega-metropolis – its property prices increasing drastically along with the popularity of lattes – the area continued to gentrify. Meanwhile in Camden the borough, the 'Britpop' bands hung out in Camden Town (the district) – down from Manchester, Oasis's Noel Gallagher lived nearby.

Today, just a few steps away from Holloway Road is Arsenal's new shiny glass and steel £390m, 60,000-capacity super stadium, the Emirates. They worked hard to keep it near to Highbury and carved the space, about 30 acres of London land, from the footprint of a waste processing plant. Nowadays the Arsenal team drives underneath the stadium to the players' entrance, out of sight and away from the crowds.

* * * *

In the early 1990s, manager George Graham had built a strong First Division-winning Arsenal side – champions in 1988/89 and again in 1990/91. They had quality and discipline and the guiding principle of defend first and keep a clean sheet, attack and get a goal if they could, then bolt the door behind them if they did. 'One-nil to the Arsenal' and 'Boring, boring Arsenal' were the chants of the era.

In 1993, Arsenal won the FA Cup and League Cup (both against Sheffield Wednesday) and a year later the European Cup Winners' Cup. Graham had players like the goalkeeper David Seaman, defender Tony Adams, forward Paul Merson and striker Ian Wright – all of them England internationals.

Adams, Merson and midfielder Ray Parlour were part of an epic Tuesday drinking club (Wednesdays often being the players' day off from training if there weren't any midweek matches). The club was seen as an opportunity for team-mates to bond and unwind and, it must be said, varying extents was little different from the drinking scenes present at other clubs at the time. Or even the England players in Hong Kong before Euro 96. At Arsenal, though, it appeared to be a little heavier: Merson had already revealed his challenges with alcoholism and later Adams would too.

As for the food ... '[A]s soon as I joined the dressing room I realised there were a lot of things wrong,' the Dutch forward Dennis Bergkamp would recall of his first impressions after joining the club from Inter Milan in 1995. 'I remember in my first season the pre-match meal would be white beans in tomato sauce, bacon, scrambled eggs ... on the coach the other players would be eating crisps and chocolate. That was England in those days.' In another interview Bergkamp would recall, 'Some players went on to the pitch burping.'

In early 1995, Graham was let go by Arsenal after it was alleged he had received bung payments for the transfers of the Scandinavian pair John Jensen and Pal Lydersen. Graham was suspended from football for a year but would later go on to take over the reins at Leeds United. By the summer of '95 Bruce Rioch, who had just led Bolton Wanderers to the Premier League from the First Division, replaced Graham. The fifth-place finish he oversaw in 1995/96 failed to inspire, however.

Booze and crisps and chocolate. Bungs then Bruce Rioch. One man, however, believed that something had to change at the famous old football club.

* * * *

I take the tube to Green Park station and the West End. When you walk out at street level, the famous Ritz hotel is nearly next door. Further along into Mayfair is a quiet street of expensive townhouses, pristine on the outside with plants on the windowsills and garages underneath that possibly contain Bentleys (which seem to be everywhere, driving about). I eventually find the address I'm looking for and wait a moment before ringing the doorbell.

Probably this is the most expensive house I've ever been inside, millions of pounds I would imagine. Inside there's a lift (a lift!), some art on the white walls and countless family photos showing lives well lived. In the lounge is David Dein, 76, sat back and sunk slightly into his sofa. With smart, greying hair, immaculate suit and tie, one leg crossed over the other, he is getting on for four decades in the football business.

David Dein grew up in the 1940s in Golders Green, about six miles north-west of Highbury, and attended his first Arsenal game when he was eight. His working life began in Shepherd's Bush as a market trader. He learned the value of what he bought and sold, how to negotiate and arrive at a price that would satisfy both buyer and seller. Later he turned to commodity trading, primarily sugar, and built up a thriving business. In 1983, he spent £292,000 buying nearly 17 per cent of Arsenal Football Club. Over the years his shareholding would reach 42 per cent before later falling back to his original 17 per cent.

Throughout his time with the club Dein would emerge as one of the game's great innovators. With Arsenal part of the 'Big Five' of the 1980s and early 90s, Dein had pushed for the creation of the breakaway Premier League. He could see what was, or at least could be, coming along on the horizon in terms of football's potential commercial direction. On trips to America he attended NFL games and liked what he saw, embracing the idea of football being a part of the entertainment industry. He brought ideas back with him to England, to Arsenal and to Highbury, acknowledging that the fans – the paying customers who attended games – should enjoy all of the matchday experience. In 1993, giant screen scoreboards were installed at the ground. Toilets and catering facilities were improved. Women and families found at Highbury a more hospitable and habitable environment. For Dein it was all about spectacle in comfort.

'We needed to change,' he explains. 'Football in the 1980s was in trouble, big trouble. There was hooliganism, fighting inside the grounds, fighting outside of the grounds. The stadia themselves were antiquated. Attendances were dropping like a stone. Women weren't going to the games. Mothers didn't want their children to go to the games. They were worried about their safety.

'When I joined the board of Arsenal in 1983, football was not in a good place. It's difficult to believe now when there is football on television every day of the week, but in the 1980s television pulled the plug on football for six months. They didn't want to be associated with the product. Something had to change. Tragically in 1989 it changed for the worst with the Hillsborough disaster. Ninety-six people lost their lives. Hillsborough was probably a catalyst for a major rethink and ultimately the creation of the Premier League.

'You have to say that going to the games in the 1980s was a fairly dismal experience. You arrived at the ground at five to three, left at quarter to five and apart from the game itself there was very little to stimulate the supporter. I wanted to change that. I wanted to take an example from America, the land of the big sell, and make football a family entertainment event. I thought we could do a lot more with hospitality and basic amenities like toilets and decent food outlets. We wanted to make it more comfortable for the fans. That was very much foremost in my mind.'

Dein was there on the Arsenal board in 1986 when George Graham was appointed manager and he was there in '95 when he was sacked. Graham's successor, Bruce Rioch, hadn't been Dein's first choice. Instead, he'd had eyes on someone else, a man unknown to most people in this country who at the time was managing in Japan. Things were about to change at the club.

* * * *

Arsene Wenger's career as a player in France had been unspectacular, finishing up with Strasbourg before moving into management with Nancy in 1984. Later, he won the French league with Monaco. He wore glasses, he was intelligent (having studied Economics in Strasbourg) and spoke five languages. He knew about diet and player conditioning and had learned how an astute approach in these areas could bring advantages over opponents. In 1996 he was managing Nagoya Grampus Eight in the Japanese J. League. During his time there he had become more zen, explaining how he 'became more tolerant, more understanding than I had been'. Over the years David Dein had gotten to know Wenger well.

'If we turn back the clock,' recalls Dein, 'I first met Arsene in 1989. It was a chance meeting while he was visiting London. He had come to watch a game at Highbury and there he was in the hospitality area. Just by himself, wearing a trench coat and these big National Health-style glasses. We got talking. I asked him how long he was in London for and he replied only for that night. I asked him what he was doing that evening. "Nothing," he said. So I said to him, "Would you like to come out to dinner with my wife and me?" He immediately said, "Yes, I would love to." That answer changed all of our lives.

'From then on we became good friends. He was the manager at Monaco at the time and since I used to go there quite often, he invited me to the games. I learned a lot about him. He was intelligent and he had an encyclopaedic knowledge of players from around the world. He had also studied sports medicine, so understood the physiology of an athlete. He was a fully rounded character, I thought. I was able to see how he interacted with the players, fans, press and the directors. He was a class act. Although he didn't know it at the time, he was auditioning for the Arsenal job. He was different to anybody I'd ever met in football, a different kind of manager, albeit he was unknown in England.

'After George Graham left in 1994, I proposed to the board that we should bring in Arsene, but I was out-voted. The board were nervous and thought we needed a manager with knowledge of English football. Eventually, we appointed Bruce Rioch.

'It didn't work out with Bruce and fortunately I was still in touch with Arsene, who by then had gone to Japan. I propositioned him, telling him that we felt the club would be more receptive now after the difficult experience with Bruce. Happily, he agreed to come although not until that October.

'In life I have a personal motto, the motto of the turtle: you don't get anywhere unless you stick your neck out! We stuck our neck out with Arsene and the rest is history.'

Rioch was relieved of his duties ahead of the 1996/97 season and the rest of the Arsenal board now agreed to go with Dein's man. On the day of his appointment the headline of the *London Evening Standard* read 'ARSENE WHO?'

'I remember the day he arrived,' says Dein. 'I went down to the training ground and told the players that we were going to announce a new manager that day. Ray Parlour asked, "Who is it going to be?" I replied, "Arsene Wenger." "Who the fuck is that?" Ray said.'

When Wenger did arrive and first met the players some of the reactions were similar to Parlour's. From club captain Tony Adams, 'At first I thought, "What does this Frenchman know about football? He wears glasses and looks more like … a schoolteacher." And from striker Ian Wright, 'My immediate impression, before he'd even said anything, was, "How can this man be a football manager?" He didn't even look like a football man! I was seeing this very tall, very thin man with this very big, ill-fitting jacket and great big glasses. I didn't know anything about him … Who is this guy?'

It wouldn't take long, though, for the positive influence of the new man to take effect. Wenger brought a change in approach to diet, physical preparation and fitness, and would empower and trust in his players, keep training focused and interesting, timed and scientific. The results would be transformative and success would follow. Ultimately his ideas and impact would prove revolutionary, not just on the club he managed but across the game as a whole and the rest of the Premier League.

* * * *

The bacon and the crisps and the burping would be phased out. In the players' canteen, where before there had been steak, chips, beans and ketchup, there would now be boiled chicken and vegetables, rice and fish. To help build muscle, supplements such as Creatine were introduced. New physical activities were encouraged such as yoga along with stretching sessions to improve the players' flexibility. In 1996, this was a fairly alien concept to the professionals at the club, and indeed across the Premier League. But those who followed Wenger's methods would see their performances improve and their careers prolonged. This was particularly the case for the club's older defensive guard of Adams, Steve Bould, Lee Dixon and Nigel Winterburn, each of whom would play into their late 30s.

Wenger was careful to manage the introductions. The chocolate was phased out, as was the jar of sweets that had sat on the dressing room table before matches. As one of his players would explain of that particular adjustment, 'He didn't take the sweets away the next day, he didn't kick up a fuss, but he invited a dietician to speak to the players and explain that sugar was not good for energy levels. Through a whole range of explanations, Arsene was able to modify these habits.'

Pretty much straight away the alcohol had gone. Captain Adams' abstinence had helped. Having informed his team-mates shortly before Wenger's arrival of his challenges with drink, Adams was simultaneously embarking on a clearer and healthier personal path. There would be advantages for others who could curtail their drinking, too. Ray Parlour noted the benefits of this particular shift, 'The old attitude wasn't good enough. Football was changing, more foreign players were coming into different teams, and the whole scene was being transformed. You had to be more on the ball … [and] if you are marking someone who's not got up to what you've got up to all week [drinking pint after pint of lager in the pub], they are going to make a fool out of you.'

Improved diet, sports science, less alcohol; with plenty of hindsight, these specifics appear obvious moves for a professional sporting organisation and its players to make. Yet at a time when others weren't doing so – either to any extent or even to a lesser degree – the advantages that were available to those that did adopt such approaches could be significant.

Before he arrived at the club, Wenger had also arranged some new signings for his team. He identified AC Milan's young French midfielder Patrick Vieira as a prospect and Arsenal signed him for £3.5m. Vieira had been with Milan for a year but had yet to win a regular place in their first team. Aged just 20, he would prove one of Wenger's most astute signings as he settled into the heart of the Arsenal midfield, emerging quickly as a pivotal player. Another addition was Remi Garde, who, having arrived at Highbury before Wenger on a free transfer from Strasbourg, had acted as his eyes and ears in the dressing room prior to his new manager's move over from Japan. Each day before Wenger arrived the two talked on the phone.

Asked about his approach to the game itself, Wenger would explain, 'I like real, modern football … football of quick, co-ordinated movements with a good technical basis.' His training sessions were intensive but varied, with short sharp exercises to keep his players engaged – quite a contrast to the regimented days of George Graham and 'Boring, boring Arsenal'. For Paul Merson, ultimately to be moved on to Middlesbrough in 1997, training under Wenger was fun. 'All the lads were getting in early for work,' he would say. 'People were flying into training at nine o'clock in the morning, it was that good to train … all 15-minute stuff so you don't lose concentration … it was brilliant.'

Striker Ian Wright would explain a further important aspect of Wenger's approach, 'He created a calming atmosphere that allowed us to think for ourselves instead of being yelled at … he was treating us like adults.' Wright would add, 'he didn't waste words, but he said what was needed to be said; and he put it across with a straightforwardness and a passion.'

This level of serenity was pretty different to what might have been seen from the typical 90s football manager in England of the time, particularly those of the old school. Footage of Leyton Orient's John Sitton in the 1995 documentary, *Orient: Club for a Fiver*, in which he regularly berates his players in the dressing room, marks the contrast. At half-time during a game at Brentford, with his team trailing 3-0, he tells them, 'You're a fucking disgrace,' before sending them out for the second half, 'Fuck off out on the pitch, the lot of you.' Also there is the 90s clip of Neil Warnock, then manager of Huddersfield Town, who castigates his players as they trail away in the rain at Shrewsbury, calling his players 'soft as shit'.

'For Arsene it was a calm and intellectual transition overall,' believes David Dein. 'He gradually introduced new training methods and dietary controls that the players accepted.'

'There was a risk that they would reject me and my methods,' Wenger would reflect about the initial changes he was working to implement. 'It would have been very easy for them to shut me out ... [But] I am proud that they listened to what I had to say and trusted me.'

* * * *

His first game in proper charge of Arsenal came in October 1996, a 2-0 win against Blackburn at Ewood Park. Wenger began with a 3-5-2 formation, the same that several other clubs were playing at the time, most notably Liverpool. He would keep that system for the rest of the season as he guided his Arsenal to third place in the table.

For 1997/98, more significant changes were made to his playing squad. Merson left for Middlesbrough and in came Ajax's Marc Overmars, the rapid Champions League-winning left-winger joining for a £6m fee. Central midfielder Emmanuel Petit arrived from Monaco for £3.5m to sit beside Vieira in the middle of what would become a formidable unit. Another Monaco player, Gilles Grimandi, also arrived for £2.5m. Both Petit and Grimandi had previously worked under Wenger in France. The striker Christopher Wreh (cousin of AC Milan 90s great and future president of Liberia George Weah) cost £500,000 from Monaco. Luis Boa Morte was a £1.8m capture from Sporting Lisbon who further increased Arsenal's attacking options. Nicolas Anelka, an explosive yet clinical clinical young striker, had already been signed from Paris Saint-Germain in early 1997 for £500,000.

On the opening day of the season at Leeds, Wenger moved away from the 3-5-2 and lined up his Arsenal side in a 4-4-2, 4-2-3-1 or 4-3-3 formation: Seaman; Garde, Grimandi, Steve Bould, Nigel Winterburn; Parlour, Vieira, Petit, Overmars; Wright and Dennis Bergkamp. Tony Adams, Martin Keown and Lee Dixon were injured for that game, which was drawn 1-1.

By now the identity and style of Wenger's Arsenal was developing; they were a stern proposition at the back, increasingly dominant in the middle of the field while pacy and clinical upfront. And all the while players were becoming stronger and healthier. As Ian Wright would recall, 'We were eating the food, taking the tablets and doing the exercises ... we realised we were getting stronger and recovery on the day after the game was so much easier. I felt fitter, sharper, faster than I'd ever been. We all were.'

The wins against Chelsea at Stamford Bridge (3-2), Manchester United at Highbury (3-2) and Newcastle at St James' Park (1-0) stood out during the early stages of the 1997/98 season under Wenger. Progress was being made.

Change, though, takes time and by mid-December '97 Arsenal still sat ten points behind Manchester United in the Premier League table.

Architects of Space

Back in the summer of 1995, Arsenal had made a progressive move when as they signed Dennis Bergkamp from Inter Milan for a club-record £7.5m fee.

Bergkamp, who would be paid a reputed £25,000 a week, was an exceptional talent – a forward who operated as a second, deeper-operating striker. He had progressed through the youth system at Ajax. Along with Eric Cantona and Roberto Baggio, he was another one of the 1990s' great goal-makers.

Bergkamp had not enjoyed his time in Italy, the rigidity and conservativeness of Inter's play failing to chime with his own instinct to advance and create, and he wanted out. When the opportunity arose to play in the Premier League, a stage on which he believed he could find space and drift between those lines, he took it.

'I remember Dennis's agent rang me to ask whether we'd be interested in him,' David Dein explains of how the move came about. 'I was keen but had to convince Bruce Rioch. I went over to Milan to negotiate the deal. Dennis was a footballing genius, so gifted, much of which was to do with his upbringing at Ajax. He was an extraordinary talent and the negotiations were not easy. In the end we agreed a figure of £7.5m. We thought he could improve the squad and enhance the team.' Also signed that summer by Arsenal was David Platt, £4.75m bringing him back to England from Italy and Sampdoria.

Bergkamp would later recall learning about the deal being agreed on the BBC's pre-internet Ceefax news service, via the headline 'BERGKAMP JOINS ARSENAL'.

Bergkamp was a model professional. He looked after himself physically and dedicated hours to his continuing development at the training ground. On a matchday he scored magical goals: note the strikes at Leicester City in 1997 – running into the area and bringing down a ball from Platt, taking one touch to cushion and control, another to cut back and take out the defender, another to set up the finish and one more past the keeper – and in Marseille against Argentina at France 98. But it was his vision and creativity that particularly made him stand out. As Bergkamp would explain, 'In my mind the idea is, make it a fantastic pass.'

In David Winner's essential book on Dutch football, *Brilliant Orange*, there is on page 56 a passage from the artist Joroen Henneman describing the beauty of a curving and defence-unlocking Bergkamp ball:

'I love it when the defenders are in a line to prevent the forward breaking through, to keep him onside. And a player plays a curved ball across the back of the defence. The defenders start to run back, but the forward, who was behind the line, gets the ball because it curls back to him. That's a miracle. Cryuff used to make passes like that and it's even nicer the way Dennis Bergkamp does it ... One moment the pitch is crowded and narrow. Suddenly it is huge and wide.'

As Ian Wright would say of his new strike partner at Arsenal, 'He made what I do easier ... the ball would always find me ... He's an architect of space.'

During his first season at Arsenal, Bergkamp took time to adjust to the Premier League, particularly its physicality. But eventually he would settle, toughen up and give as good as he got from English defenders, emerging with 16 goals in all competitions during that debut campaign.

When Wenger arrived at Arsenal in 1996, he knew that Bergkamp was waiting for him. Their meeting would be the perfect collision of two footballing visionaries and intellects – one on the pitch, the other orchestrating from the sidelines. 'As soon as he arrived,' Bergkamp would say of Wenger, 'I knew that his approach suited me.'

* * * *

Of the Premier League clubs around this time, it wasn't just Arsenal that were embracing the continental way when it came to recruitment. While Italy's Serie A still had the edge in terms of the finances available to its clubs, and therefore still had the world's best players, now thanks to the increasing riches available to English clubs, there was a surge in the number of more costly foreign talent that was brought into clubs to improve Premier League teams, and in turn the league. In particular this could be seen across the capital from Arsenal at Chelsea

At the time, Chelsea were little more than a mid-table club owned by the white-bearded Ken Bates, but they too were growing their own talented foreign legion. First in for them was Ruud Gullit, the former European Player of the Year and AC Milan star, who more recently had been playing for Sampdoria. He joined in the summer of 1995 and was handed a reported £15,000-per-week contract. As *FourFourTwo* magazine noted that summer, 'The arrival of Gullit and Bergkamp in Britain suggests that the balance of international trade in football is shifting.' After Gullit, Chelsea would sign more exotic names, several of whom had been seen in action in the Champions League or on Channel 4's coverage of Serie A.

In 1996, striker Gianluca Vialli won the Champions League with Juventus in Rome but that summer moved to Stamford Bridge on a free transfer. The Italian international midfielder Roberto Di Matteo also arrived from Lazio for £4.9m and, later, Gianfranco Zola would join them from Parma for another £4.5m (and be paid a reported £25,000 per week to do so).

Zola was the pick of the bunch. Once the understudy to Diego Maradona at Napoli, he was a diminutive ballet dancer-type, match-winning playmaker who would become a Chelsea legend. Such were his talents and his danger on the Premier League pitches, Zola would often encounter tight-marking attention from opposition defenders as he worked to unpick them. On one occasion, having been followed around all afternoon by Sheffield Wednesday's Neanderthal defender Peter Atherton, Zola was quizzed about the attention he had received all game. 'How did you like it?' he was asked. 'I prefer my wife,' was his reply.

With their expanding cast of foreign stars, Chelsea were transformed and lifted the FA Cup in '97, then in '98 the League Cup and European Cup Winners' Cup.

The trend of attracting such talent was spreading even farther across the land. In the north-east, along with Faustino Asprilla and David Ginola at Newcastle, Middlesbrough too had their own group of exotic stars. First was the tricky Brazilian forward Juninho who had arrived in England in 1995 for £4.75m from Sao Paolo. With his big smile and natural gifts for bamboozling defenders, he quickly came to be adored on Teesside – over 5,000 fans turned up to his unveiling at the club's brand new Riverside Stadium where a samba band played. 'I enjoy making the goals, dribbling two, three players and passing the ball to someone in a better position to score,' Juninho would explain of his play. Middlesbrough were funded by local millionaire Steve Gibson and managed by the respected former Manchester United captain Bryan Robson, which helps explain how a talent like Juninho found himself at the club.

In the summer of '96, they pulled off another coup in signing Gianluca Vialli's Juventus team-mate and fellow Champions League winner Fabrizio Ravanelli for £7m. Porto's Brazilian midfielder Emerson came along as well for £4m. Their recruitment, funded by Gibson and the Premier League's increasing riches, demonstrated how even less fashionable clubs like Boro could compete for such talent. As Tom Flight notes in *Yer Joking Aren't Ya? The Story of Middlesbrough FC's 1996/97 Season*, 'Suddenly it felt like everyone was capable of signing anyone … Anything was possible.'

In 1996/97 Juninho, Ravanelli and Emerson's Middlesbrough would make it to both the League Cup and FA Cup finals, losing both while getting relegated from the Premier League.

Even lower down the leagues at Third Division Wigan Athletic, there were the 'Three Amigos', the Spaniards Jesus Seba, Isidro Diaz and Roberto Martinez (the future manager of Everton and Belgium) who joined the Lancashire club in the summer of 1995.

* * * *

Late 1995 saw a significant moment for the international transfer market with the case of the little-known Belgian footballer Jean-Marc Bosman at the European Court of Justice – the outcome of which would rip up established rules in the European game, opening up the transfer market to a transformative and ultimately seismic degree.

Back in 1990, Bosman had wanted a move to French side Dunkerque after his contract had ended with his current club, RC Liege. His Belgian club had demanded that either a transfer fee four times the amount they had previously paid for Bosman be paid to them by Dunkerque; or that Bosman stay and sign a new contract worth only one-quarter of his current wage. Neither option was appealing to either Dunkerque or Bosman, so he became stranded: unable to leave while at the same time refusing to stay on reduced terms.

As an EU citizen, Bosman had the right to move across member state borders and work in other EU countries, so he took Liege to court under the 1957 Treaty of Rome for restricting his freedom of movement. 'I was held captive at my club,' Bosman would say. 'I was a European citizen and I should be able to move as freely as other workers.'

By 1995 the European Court of Justice ruled in his favour: he did have the right to move freely between member states when he became out of contract, and therefore so did any out-of-contract EU national who wished to make similar moves. And when they did move, the club that signed them would not have to pay a transfer fee for them.

Also gone now as part of the outcome of the case was the restriction on the number of foreign players allowed to play in UEFA club competition games – the limit had been three, but now there would be no restriction on the number.

These two changes combined – in particular the dropping of the three-foreigner rule – massively liberated players and widened the choice of players available to clubs. As a result, the number of overseas players brought into the Premier League would increase exponentially. Back in 1992/93 the number of non-British players playing in the opening round of fixtures of the Premier League season had been just 13, although there were more that didn't play. By 1998/99, this had grown to over 150. Famously in 1999, Chelsea visited Southampton and fielded no British players at all in their starting line-up, the first English side ever to have done so.

With their rising revenues from broadcasting and the like, Arsenal and other teams in the Premier League saw the possibilities. Meanwhile the players (and their agents) could take their share of the riches. According to figures collated by football finance expert Kieran Maguire, the combined spend on player wages by Premier League clubs was £161m in 1995/96. The season after, when the effects of the Bosman ruling were fully in place, this increased to £214m. By 1997/98, when the Premier League's new £670m four-year broadcasting deal began, the figure would increase further to £289m.

Post-Bosman free transfer moves involving Premier League clubs included Vialli to Chelsea, Steve McManaman to Real Madrid in 1999 (where the ex-Liverpool forward would be paid an estimated £70,000 per week) and Sol Campbell's controversial switch from Tottenham to rivals Arsenal in 2001. In 1996, Motherwell's Paul Lambert found himself at Borussia Dortmund following his free transfer move to Germany. By the end of his one and only season with the German club, he had lifted the Champions League.

Perhaps hardest hit by the Bosman ruling were Ajax, the Amsterdam club who had conquered Europe in 1995 with their cast of young home-grown players. By mid-1997 Edgar Davids, Michael Reiziger and Patrick Kluivert had each left on 'Bosman' free transfers.

Bosman was truly a game-changer and the floodgates had been opened.

The Double

In December 1997, Arsene Wenger's Arsenal lost 3-1 to Blackburn Rovers at Highbury. The defeat was their fourth of the season in the league and left them ten points adrift of leaders Manchester United.

'As a person I do not often show my feelings, certainly not my anger,' Wenger would say of that particular result. 'But after Blackburn, I felt let down. It was a huge disappointment. I do not usually talk to the players after the game, but this time I told them what I felt. I believe they were taking things too easily.'

'You are throwing your season away,' he told them.

A key change that came after that game was how the team's new central midfield pairing of Emmanuel Petit and Patrick Vieira would operate. While both liked to push forward and attack, from now on and on a rotating basis, at least one of them would stay back to shield Tony Adams's back four as the other advanced and helped drive attacks. Petit and Vieira understood. They would work more in harmony, in tandem, and as a result Arsenal would strengthen as a whole. From then on, the defence received greater protection, while the forwards, led by Bergkamp, did the business upfield.

From that point on that season, Wenger's revolutionised Arsenal recovered and surged back into the title race. They embarked on an 18-game unbeaten run and conceded only seven goals, shutting out their opponents on 12 occasions. Even the loss of England goalkeeper David Seaman for a spell didn't halt progress. The young Austrian, Alex Manninger, signed that summer from Grazer AK, deputised for him brilliantly, keeping six clean sheets in a row.

The key win came at Old Trafford in March '98, a victory that would take Arsenal to within six points of Manchester United at the top of the Premier League, with the Gunners having three games in hand.

With 11 minutes to go at the home of the reigning champions, the game was all square, Manninger having denied United with some excellent saves. Then Marc

Overmars took on a flicked-on ball from Nicolas Anelka, headed it on to himself and ran on speedily to finish past Peter Schmeichel for the vital winner. It was a huge moment in the title race.

After that in April, United dropped points at home to Liverpool and Newcastle and Arsene Wenger's men overtook Alex Ferguson's. With three games of the season remaining, Everton visited Highbury. A win against the Merseysiders would mean the league would be Arsenal's.

That afternoon Everton were brushed aside 4-0. For the game's finale in injury time a dinked pass from Steve Bould found Adams who, having broken through, chested the ball on before hitting home a half-volley for the fourth goal. It was only the previous season that Adams had revealed to his team-mates his struggles with alcoholism, before embarking on his journey to personal recovery. Now, on the Highbury pitch that day he had capped the title win in style. 'It was a beautiful moment,' he would later recall of the goal, 'as I closed my eyes to savour it, I simply felt great calm and peace.' Arsenal were champions with two games to spare.

'This is the biggest satisfaction of my career so far,' Arsene Wenger would say. 'I am proud to be the first foreign coach to have won the championship here ... I'm so proud that we have come from behind to win it ... The title was one way to give something back for the confidence the club had in making me manager.'

A week later, the FA Cup was added with a 2-0 win over Newcastle at Wembley, Overmars and Nicolas Anelka with the goals. The Double meant an open-top bus parade from Highbury to Islington Town Hall the Sunday after the final with 200,000 Arsenal supporters turning out for them on the streets. 'Arsene had joined the previous

October and in the next full season we won the Double,' says David Dein, whose courting of Wenger had gone back to 1989. 'The headlines in the *Evening Standard* had been "ARSENE WHO?" But the players had believed in him, his training methods, his dietary methods and man-management skills. He's a football purist and he set new standards. Winning the Double in his first full season was quite remarkable.'

Wenger became the first non-British manager ever to win the English top flight. Two months later in Paris, Vieira and Petit would lift the World Cup for France.

Legacy

A year on from Wenger's Double triumph, Real Madrid agreed to pay Arsenal £23m for their then 20-year-old striker Nicolas Anelka. Doubtless the young Frenchman had all the ability and promise of a world-class player, but the fee was too significant for Arsenal to turn down.

The money paid for two things. First, another French forward, Thierry Henry, who was signed from Juventus for £11.5m. Eight seasons and 226 goals later, he had won two Premier League titles with Wenger, including 2003/04's remarkable 38-game 'Invincibles' unbeaten triumph. Second, the Anelka money paid for the club's brand new £10m training facility at London Colney, the Hertfordshire village near St Albans. Built to Wenger's precise specifications, the facility featured ten full-sized pitches with the same grass as Highbury along with state-of-the-art health and medical facilities. Here the architecture of the centre's buildings provided for light, while the landscaping of its surrounds helped with relaxation. As Wenger's biographer Xavier Rivoire would

write, it was, 'A laboratory where Wenger-style football is developed.' A place where the revolution could continue.

* * * *

Most significantly around this time, at the beginning of the new millennium, the decision was taken for Arsenal to leave their Highbury home. Built in 1913, its 38,000 capacity was simply too small now for a club of their size and the support base they had. A brand new 60,000-capacity super stadium at nearby Ashburton Grove was planned in its place, with discussions about a move having begun in 2000. During the 1998/99 and 1999/2000 seasons, they played their Champions League group matches at Wembley to help test out demand for tickets. Each game drew over 70,000 fans, so a plan for the finest of the new stadiums built in England up to that point was developed. The £390m project would be completed in 2006.

David Dein explains the reasoning behind the move. 'Highbury was the spiritual home of the club. It was where I saw my first football match when I was eight years old, standing on the North Bank, and it held very special memories for me personally. But it was a small stadium in terms of capacity and we had outgrown it. Other clubs were expanding and we were in danger of being left behind.'

At the new Emirates-sponsored stadium, matchday revenues would increase from around £1m per game at Highbury to over £3m. With total revenues of £139m in 2006/07 (the first season in the new stadium), up from £115m the previous year, and £183m the season after, the stadium would help position Arsenal as a true super club of the time.

After the new home was built, Highbury would be converted to flats and the intimate surrounds of the old ground would be no more as Wenger led the club into their new era.

In 2007, Dein would sell his remaining shares in the club for £75m to a company owned by the billionaire investors Alisher Usmanov and Farhad Moshiri (the future major shareholder of Everton). Today Dein still attends as many games as he can at the Emirates.

* * * *

In 1992 Nick Hornby released his seminal football book, *Fever Pitch*. His writing offered perspectives on the game that had rarely been seen up to that point as he passionately and intelligently presented a fan's obsession and love for his club, Arsenal. Within its pages, Hornby covers certain nuances of his own fandom, such as moving to Finsbury Park because it was nearer to Highbury than his previous house, or where he connects Liam Brady's move to Juventus in 1980 to the loss of his girlfriend to another man – 'slap-bang in the middle of the first dismal post-Brady season' – then his later depression.

The book was both a critical and commercial success, a classic of the genre, which came out at a time when the game's image was gradually improving and its appeal increasing. As *The Observer* would claim, in specific reference to the middle classes' apparent increased interest in football at the time, *Fever Pitch* would lead to 'the emergence of a new class of soccer fan – cultured and discerning'.

Actually as David Goldblatt notes of this theory in *The Game of Our Lives: The Meaning and Making of English Football*, in terms of the changing class make-up of football crowds at the matches through the 90s and beyond, this apparent shift may not actually have taken place. 'The most common assumptions about the contemporary football crowd compared to the 1980s is that it is now richer and significantly more middle class. The best available data on the crowd before 1990 shows that, in fact, a stable class structure of around two-thirds middle class and one-third working class long pre-dates the Premiership. A cluster of surveys of both the Premier League and the Football League taken around 2000 showed little change.'

There was of course that character from *The Fast Show*, Roger Nouveau, one such middle-class supporter. 'Let's talk about football,' he says in one scene in the pub. 'It's great isn't it? Great, football … Come on, the Arsenal! Ah, I love it! Go there every week, sit in the same place.'

Perhaps, then, as the journalist Simon Kuper would more simply observe, 'Hornby didn't get the middle classes involved in football, but he allowed them to talk about football in their books and newspapers.'

During the Wenger years, Hornby remarked, 'To own a season ticket during that time was heaven, a passport to the best football in Britain, occasionally to the best entertainment in London.' My ticket today for Premier League football in 2018 at the new Arsenal stadium cost me £43.

Outside the new stadium, just five minutes' walk from Arsenal tube and Avenell Road, I count five statues of Arsenal figures placed around the wide outside concourse – among them Herbert Chapman and Dennis Bergkamp. Walking around, I pass large posters of past players and Bob Wilson, Charlie George, David Rocastle, David Seaman. Inside there is a bronze bust of Wenger.

The Emirates is pristine, with views of north London through the windows of its large inside concourse area.

I finish my drink and walk up the stairs and out to its four-level bowl of sweeping seats, sit down at the back of the stand and watch Arsenal saunter to a 4-0 lead over Crystal Palace. Twenty-two minutes are on the clock and the German playmaker Mesut Ozil and English midfielder Jack Wilshere are running the show.

This season is the 20th since Arsenal's 1997/98 Double-winning year and will turn out to be Wenger's last as manager here. Today he is over 1,000 games into his reign and yet to announce his departure from the club (that will come at the end of the season). Stood on the touchline wearing his big padded coat, he watches on as the goals fly in. It finishes 4-2 to the Arsenal.

Wenger's last game would be number 1,235 – May 2018 at Huddersfield Town. Three Premier League trophies, seven FA Cups and more than two decades on from his arrival at the club – his north London footballing revolution was at an end. And as one of his players, Lee Dixon, would appropriately surmise of his manager's impact and influence, 'There is no doubt he changed the face of English football. He was the first. It was all him. His legacy is not only Arsenal-based. It is English football-based because of where the game was when he came in and how clubs and players operated. The physiology side of the game, the social side, training – he came in and ripped up the handbook. Everybody said, "Who is this fella?" and the next minute they were all copying him. I truly believe he pushed the button to start all of that. It is easy to lose track of the fact he was the great innovator.'

8

In Manchester – Part II

City

For five years in my 20s, I lived in the rebuilt and transformed, post-1996-Arndale-bomb Manchester. Out of the destruction had come shiny new office buildings, high-end retail and a move towards more city centre living. Some weekends I'd walk around its streets, getting to know the place and getting lost in its always-changing urban landscape. After its post-industrial slump, the city had seized its opportunity to reinvent itself, resetting to create a strong forward-thinking vision for a future that embraced a consumer-led economy. Its civic leaders thought big and strategically, engaging positively with both central government and the private sector. Then they built and built. What emerged would be the confident and swaggering metropolis that it is today.

In the 1990s, there had been the construction of the large indoor arena, plus the Bridgewater Hall for the city's Halle Orchestra. A new tram network connected the suburbs with the centre and there was the development of Salford Quays at the end of the Manchester Ship Canal, where on the wall at The Lowry Centre hangs L.S. Lowry's *Going to the Match* painting. Manchester even bid for the Olympics twice (for 1996 and 2000). They didn't win, but at least they'd had a go and would later be awarded with the 2002 Commonwealth Games.

The flat where I lived was an old brick building in the centre of town, a converted storehouse of some kind with cast-iron beams holding up the ceiling and a crane-lifting mechanism still hanging on the wall outside. It was next to the cafe where I'd get my hangover bacon butty and near to the station where I could catch the tram to work in Altrincham or a train home to Sheffield. In the other direction was Ancoats where the cotton mills once bustled and, farther along, the Etihad, Manchester City's modern stadium.

As you approach the stadium on a matchday and follow the crowds of fans in light blue and white making their way to the game, the vast Etihad complex comes into view. There are the large concourses, lots of space and those San Siro-esque curved concrete walkways that take you up to the higher stands. Here is the headquarters of the Abu Dhabi-backed Premier League super club.

City had been First Division champions back in 1968 and during the 70s competed at the top level with players like Colin Bell and Francis Lee as their goalscoring icons. Since 1923 their home had been Maine Road, sat among the *Coronation Street*-type, dark maze-like terraces in the notorious Moss Side area of the city. During the 90s, the area was notorious for drugs gangs and shootings that brought the inconvenient 'Gunchester' nickname for the city. Maine Road had character; it was a proper old football ground loved by City fans. In particular its large Kippax Stand was a lively place to be.

In the 80s, City were twice relegated to the Second Division. While their supporters did not relish such slumps, they had some fun while they were there. There was the trend of taking inflatables to the games, most notably giant bright yellow bananas. In his book *The Beautiful Game?*, the journalist and City fan David Conn describes scenes at one City away game during this era, 'At a midweek game at West Brom ... fans wandered into the away terrace, the Smethwick End, with whatever they had grabbed from their kids' toy boxes: inflatable alligators, hammers, dinosaurs. When one guy finally, after several tries, managed to land his blow-up dolphin in another fan's paddling pool, a huge cheer went up. The crowd started singing, "Paddling pool, paddling pool, paddling pool", and on it went.'

When City returned to the First Division in 1989, the season's highpoint was a 5-1 victory over rivals Manchester United. In their team that day were a promising and exciting group of lads, including Paul Lake, David White, Andy Hinchcliffe, Steve Redmond and Ian Brightwell, all of whom had graduated to the first team after winning the FA Youth Cup in 1986. Alex Ferguson would call the 5-1 defeat the 'most embarrassing defeat of my management career'. The future had looked bright for City.

Under player-manager Peter Reid they finished fifth in the First Division in 1990/91 and again the following season, and the sale of the club in 1994 by the unpopular, penny-pinching chairman Peter Swales to a group led by former City player Francis Lee suggested promise. Since hanging up his City shirt, Lee had made a fortune producing toilet rolls.

Instead of the progress that had been hoped for, however, what came was regression. Early in 1993/94, Brian

Horton arrived from First Division Oxford United in Reid's place. 'Who are you?' asked one reporter at Horton's first press conference. He would only manage two bottom-half finishes during his time at Maine Road.

As their slide was taking place on the pitch, off it City were also lagging behind their peers. In 1993/94, the average attendance at Maine Road was under 27,000, the ninth-highest in the Premier League. That year they turned over just £8m (mid-table compared to the rest of the league), spending just £5.5m on player wages. By contrast, across the city at Old Trafford, Manchester United were flourishing, winning titles and trophies, attracting over 40,000 fans per game and generating over £40m in revenue.

* * * *

I first met David Conn back in 2012 when I was researching my book on Sheffield Wednesday. Conn is *The Guardian*'s football business expert who wrote the influential books, *The Football Business* and *The Beautiful Game?* Another of his titles, *Richer Than God*, charts his own relationship with City. After I'd got in touch with him he'd invited me to visit him in North Yorkshire to talk about Wednesday. A few years later, I drive up again to see him to talk about City in the 90s.

'I had started to become a journalist around that time,' explains Conn, sitting in his kitchen eating salad. 'I'd qualified as a lawyer and had worked in London but gave that up and came back to Manchester to be a journalist. I was back watching City again. I'd stood on the Kippax as a teenager, but by then I had a season ticket for a seat in the Main Stand. I went to a lot of the away games as well and was just really enjoying supporting the team. It was a good atmosphere at the time. There was finally some sort of improvement, or stability at least.

'We'd had nearly ten years of decline. We'd been relegated in 1983, which was a massive shock to City fans of my generation because we'd grown up with them being sort of a top club. We barely knew anything about that level. At the same time there'd also been this thing about us embracing failure, like a gallows humour sort of thing – the inflatables at matches, that kind of thing.

'When those kids like Lakey and David White had first broken into the team from the youth system, it had felt really positive. It really did feel like we had a close feeling for them, really wanting them to do well and being pleased and proud of them when they did. I thought we were becoming a solid club with Peter Reid. We weren't playing exciting football necessarily, but we had other good players like Tony Coton, Keith Curle, Niall Quinn. We had a decent team and there was a feeling that we were getting back to where we should be, or at least where we thought we should be. Then out of the blue they sacked Reid [four games into 1993/94] and it all seemed to turn after that.'

After Peter Reid came Brian Horton. After Horton was Alan Ball, the flat cap-wearing England World Cup-winning midfielder from 1966. Ball had managed Portsmouth and Southampton with limited success; Stoke and Exeter with even less.

Under Ball, City began the 1995/96 campaign disastrously, failing to win any of their opening 11 league games. Over four days in October they lost twice at Anfield to Liverpool – 4-0 in the League Cup then 6-0 in the league, the City fans chanting 'Alan Ball is a football genius' in sarcastic unison.

Paul Lake, one of the youngsters that had emerged from the youth system in the late 80s, remembers the feeling around the club that season. 'I knew I was watching a side doomed to fail,' he writes in his autobiography, 'and, as the season progressed, the spectre of relegation loomed ominously.' Troubled with injury for several years, Lake would be forced to retire in early 1996.

One apparent shining light of that period was Georgi Kinkladze, a 22-year-old Georgian attacking midfielder who had joined from Dinamo Tbilisi in the summer of 1995. He spoke no English but would come to dazzle and endear himself to the City fans with his skills, trickery and general likeability. 'Kinkladze was definitely something different,' says Conn. 'As a player he was just an absolute dream. He was incredibly skilful and some of the goals he scored were brilliant. The one against Southampton [in March 1996] when he went through everyone and chipped it over Dave Beasant from about six yards out – what a goal that was. We really loved him.' Despite his attacking skills, however, Kinkladze was an individualist. City's play would go through him, as his manager Ball required. Yet his lack of instinct to track back and contribute defensively weakened the team as a whole and he went missing in matches.

* * * *

During the penultimate weekend of 1995/96, the 'Britpop' leaders and local group Oasis played two sold-out gigs at Maine Road. Noel and Liam Gallagher's band had earlier emerged with the huge track 'Columbia' and the album

Definitely Maybe. In one early photo shoot, the City-supporting brothers wore the City shirts that featured the logo of the electronics manufacturer, Brother. 'Hello, Manchester. Ya all right?' said Noel when he took to the Maine Road stage. Their second record, *(What's the Story) Morning Glory?*, would go on to sell over 20 million copies worldwide.

The day Oasis played the first of their Maine Road gigs, City won 1-0 at Aston Villa after the Northern Irish midfielder Steve Lomas grabbed the winner in Birmingham. Going into their last game of the season at home to Liverpool, City still sat in the relegation places and in order to stay up they needed to better the results of Southampton or Coventry; all three teams were level on points, but City were behind the other two on goal difference. Liverpool were in the FA Cup Final the following week and with one eye on that game produced a pretty average performance. Without doubt, City were offered a good opportunity to keep themselves in the Premier League. Still, the hosts went into the half-time break 2-0 down.

In the second half, City managed to rally to bring it level, 2-2. With only a short time to go, and believing that Southampton were now losing and that a draw would be enough for them to stay up they began to run down the clock. According to Lomas, 'He [Alan Ball] called me over and said, "We're up, kill this game off, just do whatever you can."' Lomas took the ball into the corner and Ball – flat cap on his head – looked on. The problem was, Southampton weren't actually losing. City still needed another goal.

After an hour, striker Niall Quinn had been substituted by Ball. He had showered, changed and returned to City's bench area. 'I had a radio and knew that Southampton were winning elsewhere, so we needed to score,' Quinn would recall. 'I had to run down the sideline and scream at Steve Lomas that we needed another.'

Quinn's efforts would prove futile as it stayed 2-2 and City dropped out of the Premier League on a confusing and hapless goal-difference whimper. 'We went down with farce,' says David Conn.

After relegation, City slid further still, stuttering and struggling in the First Division instead of returning to the Premier League. The club had a bloated squad – up to around 40 professionals on the books around that time, a legacy of one manager after another bringing in their own players – and the team was used to losing. Despite backing from big crowds at Maine Road that season down in the First Division (26,753 was the average attendance), City simply lacked the spirit and the fight.

The demise continued through 1997/98 as they lost 22 games out of 46 and were relegated again, this time to the Second Division. As Conn would write of this period in *Richer Than God*, 'In those two years of flapping [1996/97 and 1997/98], I struggle to remember a single match in much focus.' What he would remember, though, was 'a full but indignant, neurotic Maine Road'.

For 1998/99 in the Second Division, City would be managed by Joe Royle, previously seen leading Everton to FA Cup success in 1995. Royle had replaced Frank Clark the previous season (Clark had replaced Phil Neal, who had stood in for Steve Coppell, who had picked up from Asa Hartford, who had held the fort after Alan Ball, who had left three games into 1996/97). Royle hadn't been able to steer City away from relegation, but he would turn out to be the right man for the job.

In '98, Royle revamped the squad. The individualist Georgi Kinkladze was gone and a side more suited to the ruggedness of the Second Division was built. The opening game of the season at Maine Road attracted a crowd of over 32,000 against Blackpool and around 14,000 season tickets had been sold. Promotion was expected.

We're Not Really Here

Nicky Weaver was just 18 when Manchester City paid Mansfield Town £100,000 for the young goalkeeper in 1997. Although he had only played once before for Mansfield, at the start of the 1998/99 campaign Royle was confident enough to throw him into the City first team for their opening game. Weaver is a Sheffield Wednesday fan and nowadays coaches the keepers at Hillsborough. One afternoon at Wednesday's Middlewood training ground, he recalls at his emergence in the City team.

'The move to City came out of the blue really,' he says, sitting in the press conference room. 'It was a huge club and for the first year I was there as third choice. When Joe came in, it was a bit of a mess really. There were players everywhere, something like 40 pros. Too many. He wanted to try and bring the younger ones through, the hungry ones. When they got relegated from the First Division to the Second, that kind of drew a line in the sand. It was the chance to clear the decks and start again.

'I had a year playing in the reserves and training with the first team. It was at the start of the second season that my career kick-started. There were 32,000 at Maine Road [for the Blackpool game]. I was young and very nervous. I couldn't eat my pre-match meal. We won 3-0 and I had an okay game for a debut and I never looked back from there, really.'

The Second Division was proving a big challenge for City, however, as they managed just seven wins from their opening 21 games of the season.

'It was difficult,' Weaver recalls. 'Everybody raised their game against us. It took us quite a while to adapt to that environment.'

While a promotion challenge had been the expectation for City, after defeat at York City in December the reality was 12th position in the table, the club's lowest league placing *ever.* Earlier that same month Mansfield had knocked them out of the Auto Windscreens Shield at Maine Road – the 3,007 crowd was the lowest in the club's history for a competitive fixture. That season City fans in the stands sang, 'We are not, we're not really here. We are not, we're not really here. Just like the fans of the invisible man. We're not really here.'

'I hate this division,' Royle would say.

At the time Weaver was living in digs in Manchester, keeping the young goalkeeper's feet firmly on the ground. 'There were four of us there to start with, living with a family. The lady had a hairdressing salon in the back of their place, so people would be in there and I would just be walking about. Her son had a wheelie bin cleaning business, so on my day off I used to help him. I'd have a game on a Tuesday night or something, then the next morning I'd be doing the wheelie bins with him just to keep me occupied. He'd take me to the chippy for lunch. I lived quite a normal life really.

'When we played Stoke at home [just after Christmas '98], we were 1-0 down at half-time and tempers really got going. It kicked off a little bit in the dressing room. Players were swearing at the staff and staff were having a pop at the players. I was only young and was thinking, "This is a bit tasty for me." There were times during that season when the atmosphere at Maine Road wasn't particularly nice. Anyway, we went out in the second half and we won 2-1. After that we never looked back. We went on a brilliant run.'

City climbed the table and won 13 times over the next 22 games to recover and finish third in the table. After beating Wigan Athletic over two legs in the play-off semi-finals, a Wembley final against Gillingham awaited.

* * * *

'I'd gone to Wembley for the first time as a fan in 1991,' remembers Weaver. 'Wednesday and Man United in the League Cup Final. We won 1-0 and got promoted that year too which was brilliant. We went back again in '93 for the FA Cup semi-final against Sheffield United and won that. Chris Waddle hit that free kick from miles out in the first couple of minutes. Then we had the League Cup Final [which Wednesday lost to Arsenal], then the FA Cup Final and replay [also lost to Arsenal] which were both heartbreaking for me. I never thought that six years later I'd be there myself playing for City.

'I couldn't wait for the final and not once did I think we'd lose the game. I don't know if that was because we were in good form or because we were Man City and everybody expected us to win. But we just wanted the game to come.'

That day at Wembley Weaver sported a great 1990s boy-band blond hairstyle and City's outfield players wore the club's black and fluorescent yellow striped change kit. Floating balloons were everywhere.

'I remember the noise of the crowd and of balloons popping. It wasn't a particularly nice day, the weather was drizzly and the game was a bit dull really. I didn't have too much to do really. Not much happened until the last ten minutes.'

The first goal came after 81 minutes from Gillingham's Carl Asaba to sucker punch City. Five minutes later, they struck again for 2-0 through Robert Taylor. The game and City's promotion hopes looked to be over.

'When they scored their second, well, you're thinking that you're sort of finished,' admits Weaver.

With all hope seemingly lost, one City fan inside Wembley summed it up, 'You've let us down again, you've let us down again big time.' Many City supporters left the stadium to begin the journey north, several thousand, some believe. But suddenly there was hope.

In the last minute, Kevin Horlock pulled one back for City with a low drive from the edge of the area, but it was still 2-1 to Gillingham with only 17 seconds of time remaining. 'That goal barely got a cheer,' says Weaver. 'Then they put up five minutes for injury time which I thought was quite generous to be honest. Tony Pulis [the Gillingham manager] was going mad ... He was not happy.'

In the depths of added time, a knock on fell for striker Paul Dickov in the box. After taking a great touch to control the ball and set himself up, he struck it into the net to equalise. The roar from the City fans still inside Wembley was deafening. Those who had rushed out at 2-0 down now rushed back into the stadium. In the blink of an eye, City had pulled off an unlikely and miraculous comeback. 'I ran the full length of the pitch to celebrate,' says Weaver of the equaliser. 'It was just unbelievable.' The 30 minutes of extra time came and went with no further goals. Penalties would determine who would be promoted.

After seven spot kicks, four for City and three for Gillingham (of which Weaver saved one), the young City keeper faced Guy Butters. It was 3-1 to City. Make another save and they would win and go up.

'When Guy stepped up I remember thinking, "He's left-footed. I've got to dive left." Luckily I got two good hands on it.' Weaver had saved. City had won it.

Weaver ran off in crazy celebration, his arms flapping in the air before he was caught then piled on by his team-mates. 'After I'd saved it, I sort of pulled an expression on my face. Then I just remember waving the lads over. I jumped over the advertising boards and I thought, "I'll have a little run around." I had all of this adrenaline pumping through my body and I didn't want it to end. I sort of burst out of my skin, if you like. I can't really explain the feeling.'

David Conn had been at Wembley. 'I remember thinking at the time how big a moment it was for the club,' he says. 'Such a big moment of recovery after all of the struggles around that time. It really felt like a landmark, really fundamental. Like something had changed for us in the fates.'

The following season Royle's revitalised City carried straight on up through the division, winning their return to the Premier League with a second-place finish. A brief wobble followed with a drop back to the First Division, but they recovered and won back their spot a year later. They haven't dropped out again since.

In 2003 City would leave Maine Road, moving across town to the City of Manchester Stadium, now known as the Etihad Stadium. In Moss Side, where Maine Road had stood, there would be a new housing estate with nods to the past with roads names like Trautmann Close (in honour of City's German goalkeeper who broke his neck in the 1956 FA Cup Final but played on to the end), and Blue Moon Way (in homage to City's anthem played before games). From 2008, there would be the start of the billion pounds-plus investment from the Abu Dhabi United Group that has transformed City into the club it is today: all shiny and moneyed with four Premier League titles and counting.

'I played over 200 games for City but no one talks about any other game,' explains Weaver as we finish our talk. 'They only talk about Wembley and that's fine with me. I didn't realise the magnitude of it at the time. Some people say it's the biggest win in the club's history, setting them off back up towards the top. It's something I'm very proud to have played my part in.'

Looking for Eric

March 2018. Manchester United v Swansea City at Old Trafford. The season is drawing to its end. I park the car in Stretford, about half an hour's walk from the ground. There are still a few hours to go until kick-off but I join the increasing number of people already heading over. At Sir Matt Busby Way there's the scarves and t-shirts stalls. A tenner for an 'Eric the King' Cantona French flag which I buy and stuff into my coat pocket.

Today, Old Trafford's capacity of 75,000 makes it the largest club stadium in the country, one that is full of history with it many links all around to its past. The statues of club legends Busby, George Best, Denis Law and Bobby Charlton. The Munich clock, stopped at four minutes past three o'clock when the 'Busby Babes' perished on the Munich runway in February 1958. The museum too.

On the way over I'd picked up one of the fanzines, *United We Stand*. Inside there's a piece on the club's changing fan base and Old Trafford crowd that notes how back in the late 1960s the average age of the fans on the Stretford End was 18; by 2008, that figure had more than doubled to 40. The writer laments the 'passive seat-fillers in a previously raucous stadium' and worries about an even more passive, even less raucous future at the games. Absent from the 'Stretty', he explains, is the 'excited, self-consciously self-confident bluster of young lads'.

In the early 1990s, the proportion of youngsters like that going to the football was around 20 per cent. By the mid-2000s, this had approximately halved. Increasing ticket prices suggest an explanation. At Old Trafford, the average cost of entry in 1989/90 had been just under £5. By 1994/95, this had risen to £16. Through the rest of the 90s and beyond, these prices continued to rise. '[W]e now have a young underclass who don't benefit from the ballast of the matchday experience,' the fanzine article concludes.

My ticket today, a 'borrowed' season ticket for £25 from the friend of a friend, is up in the new Stretford End. Save for a few people in the front rows, everyone is standing up. Near to me loads of people are making a good effort at getting the singing and chanting going to create an atmosphere. Not many selfies being taken up here as far as I can see. The repertoire of songs feature references to the past, to Busby and to Best, to Cantona.

Down on the Old Trafford pitch United have the £300,000-a-week Alexis Sanchez and the £90m man Paul Pogba. They comfortably sweep aside struggling Swansea,

2-0. Then I leave early, as loads of other people do. I definitely want to beat the traffic home.

* * * *

In 1997, just after Manchester United had again won the Premier League title, they lost their talisman Eric Cantona as he announced his retirement from professional football. He was only 30 and the shock of his decision had left United fans heartbroken. Some of them gathered on the forecourt of Old Trafford to be together as they grieved. The impact he had had on Alex Ferguson's team – the final piece of the jigsaw who would spur on the club to four Premier League titles in five seasons, plus two FA Cups – had been seismic.

As Philippe Auclair surmised in his book, *Cantona: The Rebel Who Would Be King*, 'He had often acted on impulse, a leaf carried by the wind of his enthusiasm, his grudges and his disappointments, but not this time ... Football was over for him. He had decided to retire, to quit at the top.' As Cantona himself had said, 'I didn't want to play anymore, I'd lost the passion.'

His lasting legacy as a United legend is captured in Ken Loach's moving 2009 film, *Looking for Eric*. In it Cantona, playing himself, comes to the aid of a struggling postman and United fan, also named Eric.

'Is that really you?' asks postman Eric when his hero appears before him. 'Yeah,' says Cantona.

'Say summat in French then.'

'Je suis Eric Cantona.'

Depressed and lost and consumed by a past love, postman Eric has also been priced out of Old Trafford. 'I miss the games, me,' he says in the film. 'It's gotta be a

good ten years now since I last went to a game.' In another
scene he recounts one part of a recent therapy session,
'You know what he asked me? "When's the last time you
was happy?"' The film then cuts to footage of Cantona
returning to the United team following his post-kung-fu
kick ban against Liverpool in 1995; and then to postman
Eric and his mates on a coach singing and drinking as they
travel to an away game.

Later, he remembers one of Cantona's magical United
goals, against Sunderland at Old Trafford in 1996 – a
sublime chip from the edge of the area that glided into the
top corner. 'Remember Sunderland?' he says. 'Ah, that was
a beauty. *Magnifique*. It was like a ballet, a dance. Kept me
going for months that goal … just sort of fills you up so
much that you just forget the rest of the shit in your life just
for a few hours.'

Not for Sale

Without Cantona there would now have to be another way
for Manchester United. Fortunately, though, Ferguson still
had a fine side at his disposal. The senior group of Peter
Schmeichel, Denis Irwin, Roy Keane, Gary Pallister, Andy
Cole were there. So were the two Norwegians signed the
previous season, defender Ronny Johnsen and poaching
striker Ole Gunnar Solskjaer. Meanwhile, 'The Class of '92'
group of Paul Scholes, Gary and Phil Neville, Nicky Butt,
Ryan Giggs and David Beckham were all now established
members of the squad.

That summer Beckham had arrived home after his
sending-off for England against Argentina in the World
Cup following his kick at Diego Simeone in Saint Etienne.
Beckham was hounded by the English press, but on his

return to Manchester his manager had rallied behind him, Ferguson being the first to call him after the incident. 'Son, get back to Manchester,' he had told him. 'You'll be fine.' In 1999 Beckham would marry the 'posh' Spice Girl Victoria Adams.

Further up the pitch for United, to try to fill the gap left by Cantona, Ferguson brought in Teddy Sheringham, then aged 31, from Tottenham for £3.5m. In terms of his linking playing style, Sheringham was a prudent and logical replacement for the Frenchman.

There would be no third Premier League title in a row that season, however. No trophies at all in fact. Having led the table from October to April, in the end they were caught by Arsene Wenger's revolutionised Arsenal. The loss of Keane for most of the season through injury had proven a significant blow, while in the Champions League they were eliminated by Monaco at the quarter-final stage.

In the summer of '98, United and Ferguson invested heavily in new players. Pallister, now 33, left for Middlesbrough following nine years' service and £10.5m was spent on his replacement, PSV Eindhoven's giant centre-back Jaap Stam. Another £4.4m went on the Swedish winger Jesper Blomqvist, then £12.6m for Aston Villa's Dwight Yorke completed a quartet of forwards with Cole, Solskjaer and Sheringham. United had had a strong make-up before the arrival of their three new players, but now not only did they have options but also depth and quality across the whole squad. This would prove key for what would turn out to be a 60-plus game campaign. 'I had pushed through the improvements to the squad that I saw as being essential if we were to have a successful season,' Ferguson would comment on that summer's transfer business.

* * * *

By the end of the previous 1997/98 campaign Manchester United were a £88m turnover football club-business that posted profits of almost £30m. Revenues from matchdays and commercial operations exceeded £72m as their then 55,000-capacity Old Trafford sold out week after week. And shares in United, which were traded on the London Stock Exchange, appeared a good investment. But any party managing to get hold of the plc's millions of shares, would be able to launch a full takeover bid. In September 1998 that's what happened when BSkyB, the media company that owned Sky TV – which broadcast the Premier League in England, and which itself was owned 40 per cent by Rupert Murdoch's News International – launched a £623m approach.

In 1998, Andy Walsh was 36 and had been going to Old Trafford for over three decades. He had lived through the changes of the nascent Premier League era and had celebrated the triumphs that came United's way during that period. He'd seen the standing areas go and had been squeezed ever more tightly for his money for the rising ticket prices for matches. He'd had his Saturday afternoon routine disrupted by kick-off days and times changed to suit broadcasting schedules. He was massively opposed to the BSkyB Murdoch bid.

Back in his Stretford living room, where earlier we'd talked about Cantona and league titles, he now explains his objections to the bid and what he and a group of fellow supporters did next.

'The reason I was against the Murdoch bid was because things had gone too far already. And then here was an organisation that previously had had no real links with the football club but were now looking to come in and take it over completely. For me there was a fear about that, an uncertainty over why they were doing it and what they might use the club for.

'Our opposition was instant. As soon as the announcement was made, we started talking about how we could stop the takeover. The concerns amongst supporters were widespread. Amongst the fanzines and the group I was involved in, IMUSA [the Independent Manchester United Supporters' Association], we were against it from the start. As match-going fans we felt that we were in touch with United's core support. We never claimed to represent all United fans. We only represented our members. But we did believe that we genuinely represented a large proportion of United's support.

'After these discussions we were able to build a very clear message of opposition to the Sky bid, one which we believed at its root held an authentic message of the match-going fan. It wasn't long after that that we were able to build a well-structured and well-organised campaign.'

Their fight – one that would take their opposition to the bid all the way to the Monopolies and Mergers Commission – would run from September 1998, when BSkyB made its bid, until the following spring.

'I think that early on we had the humility to recognise we didn't have all of the skills we needed within our own ranks,' explains Walsh. 'But the United fan base is a massive pool of people and we were able to call on others who did have the expertise. Once we started to talk, we found that we could access experts all over the place. We knew that as a group it was important to be articulate and professional, so we started to learn how to build a successful anti-takeover campaign. We soon created a real sense of momentum.

'Of course, we knew that we were trying to achieve the impossible – beating this massive global media entity. And we weren't necessarily confident of winning. It was more a question of us doing what we saw as being the right thing. And that was what bound us together, our love for Manchester United and us not wanting the club to fall into their hands.

'I remember hearing from one of our group who went home after one of our meetings and he had told his girlfriend about what we were doing. She basically said to him, "You what? You lot are going to take on Rupert Murdoch, one of the most powerful men in the world? You're mad. What chance have you got? You've not got a grip on reality. You still think that Eric Cantona is God!"' Earlier into the campaign, during a home game against Charlton, one fan had streaked on the Old Trafford pitch with 'Takeover My …' written above his arse.

Ultimately the group's determination and professionalism would mobilise over 350 submissions to the Office of Fair Trading in opposition to the bid. 'Going through that process isn't something the general public usually gets involved in,' says Walsh. 'Gathering all of the arguments and presenting them in an authentic voice that fitted into the right framework was difficult. But we had academics, economists, lawyers, all offering their time for free. So as it developed it wasn't just a gang of raggy-arsed football fans arguing about this deal.'

Predominantly, the argument was on the grounds of it being anti-competitive for a broadcaster of a particular league that was involved in the negotiations for future rights deals, while at the same time owning one of its participant clubs. In turn, this would lead to a referral to the Monopolies and Mergers Commission which, it was hoped, would block the bid.

'Ultimately, I think that they [BSkyB] completely underestimated the backlash that came from a group of ordinary football supporters. They took us for mugs really and thought that we'd all just go for the spin of the investment without any proper thought or analysis.'

For Walsh and many others in the group, the reality of the battle was a simultaneously energising and draining experience. 'You just run on adrenaline,' he says. 'The games were an escape, of course. They were a really healthy reminder of what you we were doing it for and why you were doing it. It was all about United.'

Football, Bloody Hell

On the pitch, victory over Nottingham Forest on Boxing Day 1998 would begin a 20-game unbeaten run in the Premier League for Alex Ferguson's side. By the end of March they were top of the table, four points clear of Arsenal. In the FA Cup meanwhile, they had advanced first past Middlesbrough then, in dramatic fashion at Old Trafford, Liverpool – Ole Gunnar Solskjaer slotting in the winner in injury time after Dwight Yorke had equalised two minutes before the 90 minutes were up.

That season United played excellent attacking football, with a high and relentless energy level, and late goals were a key theme of the story. Often they were the deserved output from a team driven and determined to push on until the end in search of goals.

Over the previous two seasons, United had exited the Champions League at the semi-final and quarter-final stages, succumbing to Borussia Dortmund in 1996/97, then Monaco in 1997/98. Ferguson was frustrated with how close they were getting to success in Europe, viewing the competition as he did as his ultimate goal in management. '[A]s far as I was concerned Europe had become a personal crusade,' he would say of his quest. 'I knew I would never be judged a great manager until I won the European Cup.'

In his book, *The Mixer*, Michael Cox analyses United's tactical evolutions in Europe through the 90s, explaining how Ferguson took an interest in the different systems used by teams from other leagues, in particular Italy. Cox outlines how Ferguson learned from United's defeats in Europe and developed new ideas based on possession, discipline for specific tactical tasks (such as man-marking or more disciplined positioning) and flexibility depending on who United's opponents were. Often he would test out new ideas in the Premier League first. 'His adventures throughout the 1990s were essentially a long, gradual learning curve,' writes Cox.

In the 1998/99 quarter-final, United faced Inter Milan and advanced following a 3-1 aggregate scoreline. United won 2-0 at home and in the second leg at the San Siro, Paul Scholes struck an equaliser with two minutes to spare to confirm their progress. Ferguson had set his side up astutely, adapting and tweaking positioning to deal with the threat of Inter, and they had controlled both games.

In April, United reached the semi-final of the FA Cup. After drawing with Arsenal at Villa Park in the first tie, the replay on the same ground provided a dose of high drama. Back when clubs still chose to field their strongest teams in the tournament, that evening both sides put on a terrific show.

In the last minute, with the score at 1-1 and United down to ten men since the 74th minute following Keane's red card, Phil Neville brought down Arsenal's Ray Parlour in the box for a penalty. Dennis Bergkamp stepped up calmly for the Gunners, but Schmeichel saved and the game moved into extra time. Then came one of the moments of the season.

Having been brought off the bench after an hour to offer some fresh legs for United, Ryan Giggs intercepted the ball in his own half, ran on with it at his feet, took out the Arsenal defence before blasting it past David Seaman for a superb goal. His shirt was off, swinging around his head, as he ran around in celebration. 'There was no technique or anything,' Giggs would later explain of his goal. 'I didn't think about it … it was instinct really.' United were through to the FA Cup Final.

* * * *

Every year since 1993 the final of the European Cup had featured an Italian Serie A side, with AC Milan and Juventus each winning the trophy in the decade. During that time no English side had made it to the final. The last one to do so had been Liverpool back in 1985 and, following the Heysel ban, recovery for English clubs on the top European stage had been a long process.

In the 1999 Champions League semi-final, United faced Juventus, led by Carlo Ancelotti (who had recently replaced the great Marcello Lippi, winner of three Serie A titles and the Champions League with Juve). Juve had

...an to take hold of the ground, but this was relieved when ...ee minutes before half-time Beckham hit a powerful ...ling strike to equalise. Meanwhile in London, Arsenal ...ere still drawing. Two minutes into the second half, ...ndy Cole then put United ahead, lifting the ball over Ian ...Valker in the Tottenham goal. It finished 2-1. Despite ...Arsenal's eventual victory against Villa, the title – United's fifth Premier League crown in seven years – was won and trophy number one was lifted. The following night Roy Keane and his team-mates had a few drinks to celebrate in Manchester, got into some bother in a bar and, six months before signing his new £50,000-per-week contract with United, the Irishman spent the night in a police cell.

The following weekend it was on to Wembley for the FA Cup Final – day seven of 11 on which Newcastle United were no match for the Red Devils and were comfortably put away 2-0, Teddy Sheringham then Scholes with the goals. Two trophies from two and Bayern Munich in Barcelona were next.

* * * *

At one end of Deansgate, the long road of bars and pubs, shops and gleaming office blocks that cuts across Manchester, is the barber's I went to when I lived there. It had those big traditional barber chairs and uncomfortable wooden pews to wait on. There were three blokes and sometimes you'd get the fella with the white hair and glasses. He didn't talk much but when he did it would usually be about work or football. He was a United fan and I remember him once telling me about his travels at the end of that 1998/99 season. Probably it was a story he'd told a few times before: about how the

France's Zinedine Zidane at their disposal and in the first leg at Old Trafford, United had trailed 1-0 before Ryan Giggs equalised in injury time to level the game – another late goal. The return leg was a remarkable night of drama and fight, one that would take United one step closer to the prize Ferguson coveted most.

In Turin it didn't begin well for them as Juventus took a 2-0 lead after just 11 minutes to lead 3-1 on aggregate. A comeback of any kind appeared unlikely. But this was a tenacious and push-to-the-end Manchester United team.

On 24 minutes, Keane headed home a Beckham corner to make it 2-1 on the night and 3-2 on aggregate. Then he picked up a yellow card, which meant that had they got through to the final he would be suspended for it. A minute later Dwight Yorke equalised, heading in a Beckham cross to make it 2-2 on the night and 3-3 on aggregate. United now led on away goals.

In the second half, a foul by Paul Scholes earned him a yellow card, too, which would also have ruled him out of the final along with Keane had United made it through. With seven minutes left, Andy Cole hit the winner to make it 3-2 on the night and 4-3 overall. It was another great comeback for United – albeit not a last-minute one – in which captain Keane in particular was superb. Knowing that he would be banned for the final, he had still dominated the game (in fact he had been doing so even before his booking), stopping Juventus and instigating United's forward play to help guide them to the final. 'I was so much into this battle that the consequences of the card barely registered,' he would say.

It would be the club's first European Cup Final since 1968 and would be played in Barcelona's 90,000-capacity footballing cathedral, the Camp Nou, with German giants Bayern Munich providing the opposition.

There was just over a month of the season remaining and United had eight games to play across three competitions – two cup finals and the finale of the Premier League season. For Ferguson and the team he had built and evolved over the years – blending established stars with shrewd signings and hungry products of the club's youth system – here was the possibility of the Treble.

* * * *

In April '99, the group of United supporters that had been opposed to the BSkyB takeover of the club learned that the bid had been rejected by the Monopolies and Mergers Commission. In a statement made by Secretary of State for Trade and Industry, Stephen Byers, it was announced that the offer was to be emphatically blocked on the grounds of competition, both in broadcasting and the British football industry.

'[I]n order to protect the public interest I am blocking the proposed merger between BSkyB and Manchester United,' Byers said. Additionally, he noted the deal's potential to 'damage the quality of British football by reinforcing the trend towards growing inequalities between the larger, richer clubs and the smaller, poorer ones'. All of the work and campaigning since the previous September by Andy Walsh and his fellow United supporters had paid off. The group had come together for one unified cause, built a sophisticated and highly organised campaign and succeeded against all the odds. BSkyB would not be buying Manchester United plc.

'It was total elation, excitement, ▮ sense of achievement when we found ▮ Walsh of the decision. 'It gave us this ▮ reaffirmation of who we were, what we stoo▮ how we had gone about it. Personally I was ▮ too. We really felt it was the right outcome.'

After the announcement there was a big ▮ in town for those that had been involved in the ▮ After that, those United fans could focus on and ▮ what was coming up for their team during the re▮ matches of the season. The announcement had c▮ the Friday before the Sunday of the first Arsenal F.▮ semi-final and in the book that Walsh and Adam B▮ released about the campaign, *Not for Sale: Manchester Un▮ Murdoch and the Defeat of BSkyB*, they wrote, 'Barely had ▮ dust settled on the grave of Murdoch's bid to buy the clu▮ than United were straight into the chase for a Treble dream▮ For many Reds, it was now like going for the Quadruple.'

* * * *

May 1999 was the end of the 1990s in British football. For Manchester United, the kings of the Premier League era, they were staring down at 11 days to potential greatness. A short period in time that promised everything for the club. So much to win and so much to lose.

Day one of 11 was Tottenham Hotspur at Old Trafford. Win the game and the Premier League would once again be United's. Draw or lose and Arsenal, playing Aston Villa at Highbury, might nip in and win it instead.

Things got off to a worrying start when on 24 minutes Spurs took the lead through Les Ferdinand. Nervousness

week after the Tottenham game at Old Trafford he'd gone down to Wembley for the FA Cup Final, then the day after moved on to Barcelona for the Champions League Final (which back then was still played in midweek). "What a life," I thought. Jammy bastard.

United themselves travelled to Spain on Concorde. They would be based in the town of Sitges where the players could relax beside the Mediterranean. Thousands and thousands of reds followed them over; over 100,000 were in Barcelona, they say, many without a ticket for the game.

Andy Walsh made the journey with some family and friends. 'I hadn't gone to Turin [for the semi-final] but obviously I was going to Barcelona,' he says. 'There was a group of us and we hired a couple of people-carriers and drove all the way down through France, to Spain and to Barcelona. I'd got tickets for my dad and my sister high up in the gods.'

Day 11 of 11

In the group stages of the Champions League that season United had drawn twice with Bayern and, as Gary Neville would later say of their final clash, 'We were confident. We never once thought that we weren't going to win.' In Barcelona the line-up for Ferguson's side would be Schmeichel in goal; Gary Neville, Ronny Johnsen, Jaap Stam and Denis Irwin at the back; Ryan Giggs on the right of midfield (instead of his usual position on the other side), Jesper Blomqvist on the left, Nicky Butt in the middle alongside David Beckham (instead of on the right); Dwight Yorke and Andy Cole up front – between them the pair had scored more than 50 times that season.

As kick-off approached, the atmosphere in the Camp Nou was electric with United fans significantly outnumbering Bayern's in the 90,000 crowd. It was Bayern that started the better, however, as they took the lead in the sixth minute through Mario Basler's free kick. The strike hit the bottom corner of the net, whizzing past Schmeichel who stood rooted to the spot. As the first half progressed, things were not going to plan for Ferguson's men.

At half-time he delivered a speech that explaining to his players in no uncertain terms what they could expect if they did not work hard for the next 45 minutes and get themselves back into the game. 'You will be six feet away from the European Cup, but you won't be able to touch it,' Ferguson told them. 'Don't you dare come back in here without giving it your all.'

Despite his rousing words, it was Bayern that had the chances to put the game to bed in the second half. On 79 minutes, Mehmet Scholl hit the bar – Schmeichel was beaten. Four minutes later, Carsten Jancker hit the crossbar. The game was slipping away from United. The story goes that George Best, scorer in the 1968 European Cup Final against Benfica at Wembley, had left the stadium to find a bar. Was there any hope for this late-scoring team?

On 66 minutes, Ferguson had replaced Blomqvist with Sheringham, then 15 minutes later Cole with Solskjaer. As the clock moved past 90 minutes, United won a corner.

Three minutes of added time had been shown on the board. Beckham composed himself quickly and swung it in. Bayern cleared but Giggs sent it back for Sheringham to roll it past Oliver Kahn to score, and United had equalised.

In the Camp Nou stands Andy Walsh, his sister and his dad celebrated wildly with the rest of the United supporters. 'It was an incredible moment when the equaliser went in,' he says, 'just a huge emotional rush. We'd been willing the players to get that goal and when they got it there was so much elation. It was incredible.

'After that was the realisation that we were still in the game.'

After the restart United won the ball from Bayern and advanced again. Solskjaer won another corner. Beckham, again, composed himself quickly and swung it in. It reached Sheringham who headed it on, where it fell for Solskjaer who stuck out his leg, connected and scored. United were ahead, right at the death.

It was mayhem in the stands for the United fans and delirium for the players and Ferguson. 'When we got the winner the sound ... it was *monstrous*,' says Walsh. 'Absolutely monstrous. Even in the area where we were that didn't have a roof on it, the noise was phenomenal. That continued on for ages and ages. The realisation of what was happening. It was just pandemonium.'

Two goals in added time and United were winning. Bayern had no time to recover and unbelievably, miraculously, United had done it. In the blink of an eye, they'd taken the trophy, the Champions League. They'd taken the Treble.

* * * *

'The celebrations begun by that goal will never really stop,' Alex Ferguson would recall of Solskjaer's winner and its aftermath. 'Just thinking about it can put me in a party mood.'

'The last minute in Barcelona, I just lay on the floor and looked at the sky,' Gary Neville would remember.

After the cup had been presented to them, United took it on a lap of honour around the Camp Nou pitch. Player after player, they took it in turns to lift the cup in front of the fans. Ferguson was lifted on to shoulders. '[T]hey never give in,' he would say of his team after the game, 'and that's what won it.'

It had been 32 years since United had last won that trophy. Liverpool had been the last English club to do so in 1984, then came the Heysel ban, all before English football's recovery and re-emergence. Now the Premier League and its best team, Manchester United, was back on top of the European stage. A full circle footballing story.

'It's hard to beat the feeling we had that night,' says Walsh. 'It was right up there as one of the great moments of my life. The emotional roller coaster of the game, of that whole season, it was surreal really. Dream-like almost. That ending was a once-in-a-lifetime experience.'

As Ferguson had famously ended his post-match interview on the Camp Nou pitch, 'Football, bloody hell.'

'After the game we found this bar with just a few locals in it and us,' remembers Walsh. 'The bar owner couldn't believe his luck. He kept it open and that night we drank them dry. It was just fantastic.'

Love United

Six years on from Barcelona and three Premier League titles later, the takeover of Manchester United plc eventually came. In 2005, the American Glazer family, owners of the NFL franchise the Tampa Bay Buccaneers, made their purchase through a controversial £790m leveraged takeover. They did it using over £500m of borrowed money with, as David Conn would report in *The Guardian* in 2015, 'about £700m in interest and other finance-related costs having been paid by the club since then.'

For Andy Walsh and many other United supporters like him, this would be the end of the journey. For them, there would be no going back to Old Trafford, the place they probably loved most in the world. No longer would they be putting their money into the business that was now owned by the Glazers. The rising ticket prices and shifting kick-off times, the rampant commercialisation of their football club and, now, their money being used to service the debt that had been taken on. For Walsh and others, after a lifetime of passionate, all-consuming support, enough was enough. No more season tickets. No more United matches. It was time to walk away.

'I remember not long after the takeover my dad and our Patrick [Walsh's son] were sat on the settee and they just said, "We're not going back." I remember saying, "But I've renewed the season tickets." Then my dad saying, "Well you'd better un-renew them because we're not going back. Not a penny more." We agreed and I wrote a letter withdrawing my season ticket renewal.

'I'll be a United fan until the day I die, but what the Premier League had become and what each of the clubs in the Premier League now are, compared to what a football club was even 20 years ago, I just didn't really recognise anymore. It's a corporate beast. That's part of why I stopped going to United.

'After the Treble season in '99 there were a lot of people around saying, "It isn't going to get any better than this. Where do you hop off?" It was getting more and more expensive. People had spent thousands of pounds that season following the team home and away and in Europe. I remember some people saying, "Well, I'm still a United fan but I just can't afford it anymore."

'It was gut-wrenching even to write that season-ticket letter. I was hugely conflicted and really upset about it all. Proper tearful really.'

Andy Walsh, the Manchester United fan who had gone to Old Trafford with his dad, then his mates. Had the paper rounds and jobs in shops to pay for the tickets. Had gotten involved in the supporters' groups. Had watched the emergence of Ferguson's dominant teams. Fought BSkyB's takeover of the club and was there for the Treble. Now he was walking away – posting the letter to split up with the club he had loved all his life.

'It really is one of the hardest things I've ever had to do,' he says. 'It seems ridiculous, but the fact that I'm getting emotional about it now must mean it still has an impact on me. I genuinely feel sick just thinking about it.

'After I'd done it, I couldn't watch United on the telly for about a year. It was like a severe loss for me. Somebody I know who had also done the same thing talked about it as being like an ex-girlfriend going off with somebody else. That they didn't love you anymore. It was like a grief but the person hadn't actually gone away. They were still there.'

In the wake of this split, Walsh and several thousand other United fans formed a new football club. Non-league and supporter-owned, democratically operated and down in the tenth level of the English football pyramid. For the 2005/06 season Football Club United of Manchester (FC United) would average gates of over 3,000, predominantly at Bury's Gigg Lane ground.

'At first I wasn't going to be involved because it was all still too raw for me,' explains Walsh. 'I was invited to attend one of the early meetings of the steering committee and I was a bit in awe really of what they'd done so far.

The people were really organised and structured and had done so much to get things moving. I just thought that I couldn't contribute anything much to it. It was already up and running and for the first couple of meetings I don't think I even spoke.'

Ultimately Walsh would get involved and become increasingly central in the operations of the new club, eventually taking the role of FC United's general manager, one he would hold for over a decade. The club would rise through the levels, winning four promotions, and by 2015 would move to their own £6.5m stadium in the Moston area of the city (only a few miles from Newton Heath where it had all begun for Manchester United back in 1878). Broadhurst Park would be home to £10-entry, standing-on-the-terraces-with-your-mates football. No sponsor on the shirt and 3pm Saturday kick-offs.

* * * *

I leave Walsh in his Stretford house and we shake hands as I say goodbye. He wishes me good luck for the book. On the way out he shows me a framed photograph that he keeps on his bookcase of football books. The photo is of Walsh sat at an IMUSA meeting, circa 1999. There's a pint of beer in front of him and a microphone nearby for questions from the crowd. Beside him is Alex Ferguson, dressed in a brown jacket, blue shirt and brown tie – there that night for the fans in the room. For Walsh, it is a fond memory for sure. 'Andy's a nice lad,' as Ferguson would describe Walsh in one of his autobiographies.

I get back in the car and make the short journey back to Old Trafford for a last walk around the ground. The high rising stands and the red doors of the turnstiles, the vastness of this Premier League empire. In late 2018, 20 years on from the Camp Nou, Ole Gunnar Solskjaer would be back here, taking over as the club's new manager, returning to try to improve the fortunes of United in the post-Ferguson era and bring some of the magic back from 1999.

I walk back to the car, throw the notepad on to the seat and leave Manchester again for home.

Epilogue

Here We Are

AT THE end of the Snake Pass road in Sheffield is a pub close to where I used to live. It sits up there in a leafy part of the city and has comfy seats and lots of TVs on the wall for the football. On Sundays, some good friends and I would spend hours in there watching the games. Super Sundays in the Broomhill Tav. Me and Jimmy and Matt.

We all went to the same school together and were all born in the 1980s. Our earlier football memories from the 1990s of Wednesday at Hillsborough or Sheffield United at Bramall Lane. Matt was a Blade, or a 'Pig' as they are known to us Wednesdayites and us to them. We'd sit there in that pub all day drinking and talking about football and life, arguing about things and being stupid. Sometimes there'd be a football quiz, prepared by Matt – serious business. Our record for football watched in one day was four games, including the Spanish one.

We lost Matt aged 33. He had his challenges. The day we found out my heart broke. In one moment a friend who was always there for you suddenly wasn't going to be around anymore.

Before then Jim had moved abroad and I don't live up here anymore. But today I'm back, just as a one-off. Matt used to call it having a 'lonely pint', meant in a good way.

On the screen is the Premier League in all its charms. One team, owned by an American, the other by a Russian – both are billionaires. The Russian's team are in position for one of the top-four places that will bring them Champions League football next season.

Down in the 60,000-capacity super stadium on the screen the green pitch is pristine – gone are the muddy and bobbly versions of the past. The play on display is tactical, cagey and precise. The game is being broadcast to over 200 countries across the world and watched by billions of football fans. Today the Premier League is a true global league and brand. Around two-thirds of the players in the league now come from overseas. The combined domestic and international broadcasting deals for the latest three-year period is more than £9bn, around £3.1bn a season to be split among the 20 clubs – a long way from the league's first £304m deal back in 1992. An adult season ticket at the home club's stadium is getting on for £700. The money from the TV and the tickets goes to the players. Today the average wage of a Premier League footballer is over £60,000 per week. One of the players in this game earns £350,000 a week, more than £18m a year. His transfer fee a few years ago was £42.5m. In 2000 the average player wage in the Premier League had been around £7,000 per week. Back when the new Premier League began it was just under £1,500.

The players now are elite performance athletes, ready to cover around 10km of running over the 90 minutes of the game. No boozing for these lads. Their play based less on physicality and power and more on space and technique, all underpinned by sports science and athleticism. Not many errors or much sloppiness here – apart from the home side's goalkeeper when he flaps at a cross that leads to a goal for the visitors.

Commentating for Sky Sports is Martin Tyler, a veteran from the first televised Premier League game in 1992, Nottingham Forest v Liverpool. Almost a decade on from retiring as a Manchester United player, Gary Neville provides the co-commentary.

* * * *

In 1999, three years after his Newcastle 'Entertainers' were beaten to the Premier League by Manchester United, Kevin Keegan became manager of the England national team. He took them to Euro 2000 in the Netherlands and Belgium and their exit came at the group stage. People said he was tactically inept and not suitable for a job at that level. His last game was a 1-0 defeat to Germany in the rain at Wembley. Afterwards, wet through and with the look of a lost man, he resigned. His replacement would be Sven-Goran Eriksson, England's first foreign manager. The Germany game would be the last match to be played at the old Wembley as it made way for a brand new, 90,000-capacity replacement, at a cost of £750m.

On New Year's Eve 1999, the Millennium Dome was officially opened for its big party night. Tony Blair and Her Majesty The Queen linked arms for 'Auld Lang Syne'. Afterwards everyone survived the Millennium Bug and in 2001 Blair would secure a second election win for New Labour. That same year the attacks of September 11 on New York and The Pentagon would bring the 'War on Terror' during which Blair would side up to American President George W. Bush – it was a long way from headers with Kevin Keegan.

Alex Ferguson – Sir Alex from 1999 following Manchester United's Treble win – would enjoy 14 more seasons at Old Trafford, winning eight more Premier League titles and another Champions League in 2008 before retiring in 2013. Five years later, Arsene Wenger would leave Arsenal after more than 20 years in charge of the club he had transformed.

In 2003 Wimbledon FC would be moved 60 miles north to Milton Keynes after an independent commission appointed by the FA determined that it was fine for them to do so. 'Football has ended,' one Wimbledon fan would say of the decision. The phoenix club AFC Wimbledon would rise through the divisions, eventually earning back their place in the Football League.

Over the decades, the immersive world of football stats and graphics, transfers and tactics of the computer game *Championship Manager* (first developed in 1992 by the Everton-supporting brothers Oliver and Paul Collyer) would evolve into a highly sophisticated simulation series. Due to its addictiveness, over the years it would be cited in numerous divorce cases.

In 2017, Ewan McGregor's Renton character updated his 'Choose life' sermon in *Trainspotting* to *T2 Trainspotting's* 'Choose Facebook, Twitter, Snapchat, Instagram … Tell the world what you had for breakfast and hope that someone, somewhere cares.' The previous year in the United Kingdom, 52 per cent of those who voted in the referendum had chosen Brexit.

Meanwhile, two decades and counting since Sheffield Wednesday were relegated from the Premier League, their exile continues.

* * * *

Up on the screen in the pub the game finishes 2-1 to the away side. I finish my pint and step outside into the early Sunday evening. Walking home I think about the book, the project, almost at journey's end. I think about the trips and the meetings, the matches and the laps of the grounds. Motorways and trains, books and old footage, listening to the folks who were there who lived through it all. 70,000 words nearly in place and ready about football's transformation from 'Old' to 'New'. The foreign revolutions and the money, the new stadiums and tactical evolutions.

Football in the 1990s.

There we were. Now here we are.

2017

Eric Cantona has a new book out. A collection of his drawings and sketches called, *My Notebook*. He is in Manchester for a signing and one Wednesday in November, in the name of research, so am I.

Inside the store and there he is. Sat down at a table. Black Sharpie in hand. Shaven head, big beard.

'Hello,' he says.

He holds out his big Cantona hand and we shake.

'Hi,' I say. 'Nice to meet you.'

'You too,' he says.

He signs the page and passes his book back to me.

'Merci,' I say to Eric Cantona.

Acknowledgements

AS EVER I am grateful to everyone who was kind enough to support me as I worked through this project. In particular, Paul and Jane Camillin at Pitch Publishing who once again backed me all the way.

After travelling around the country to spend time interviewing a brilliant cast of 1990s football people, I must thank the following individuals for their time:

Pat Allison, David Conn, David Dein, Mick Edmondson, Roy Evans, Les Ferdinand, Sir John Hall, Simon Inglis, Dale Jennins, Dave Kelly, Tony Nelson, John Robb, Kevin Sampson, Andy Walsh (cheers for the brews), Dave Watson, Don Watson and Nicky Weaver.

Trevor Braithwait at Sheffield Wednesday set up the meeting with Nicky Weaver and Matt Grace at Populous organised the chat with Dale Jennins. Simon Hughes showed me the way in Liverpool; Simon Ellis-Jones got me a ticket for the game and introduced me to Roy Evans. In Newcastle, Wendy Taylor set things up with Sir John Hall and Dave Watson (Up the Owls! Wendy). Ken Loach gave me invaluable background on *The Flickering Flame* and *Looking for Eric*. Kieran Maguire shared his comprehensive Premier League finances stats.

When the words were ready, my friends Dr David Conroy and Aaron King gave up their time to review early drafts. Richard Lapper did the same and our chats along the way helped me see the wood for the trees. Claire Wingfield and Gareth Davis expertly whipped the final version into shape.

Thanks to Philippe Auclair for writing his perfect biography of Eric Cantona and to the Collyer brothers for creating *Championship Manager* all those years ago (and to our Mum and Dad for buying us our computer to play it on). Thanks to Lauren Bravo for writing her wonderful book on those Spice Girls – it came out midway through my own journey of looking back and gave me the licence to be nostalgic every now and then. Thanks to Chris Olewicz for always being the voice of reason and to Dave Lawson for listening to me go on about the idea over a beer or two in Vegas. Thanks to our Anna for helping with some 90s memories.

Lastly, to the Tavern lads Jimmy Caruth and Matthew Halliday (1985–2018), and my pal on the North Stand who is always there, Jonathan Hill.

Cheers everyone, it's been fun. Time now to look forward again.

Bibliography

Books

Adams, Tony with Ridley, Ian, *Addicted* (CollinsWillow, 1998)

Aerofilms Guide: Football Grounds (Dial House, Various Years)

Alexander, Duncan, *Outside the Box: A Statistical Journey Through the History of Football* (Century, 2017)

Armitage, Simon, *All Points North* (Viking, 1998)

Armstrong, Gary, *Football Hooligans: Knowing the Score* (Berg, 1998)

Auclair, Philippe, *Cantona: The Rebel Who Would Be King* (Macmillan, 2009)

Aughton, Peter, *Liverpool: A People's History, Third Edition* (Carnegie Publishing, 2008)

Baggio, Roberto, *Una Porta Nel Cielo: Un' Autobiografia* [A Goal in the Sky: An Autobiography] (Limina, 2001)

Bale, John, *Sport, Space and the City* (Routledge, 1993)

Barton, Wayne, *You Can't Win Anything with Kids: Eric Cantona, Manchester United and the Incredible 1995/96 Season* (Empire Publications, 2016)

Bergkamp, Dennis with Winner, David, *Stillness and Speed: My Story* (Simon & Schuster)

Binns, George, Hodgson, Alan, Thomas, Owen and Thomas, Ian, *100 Years: All That's Worth Knowing – Facts and Photos – Huddersfield Town A.F.C. Centenary History* (Huddersfield Town Football Club, 2009)

Bower, Tom, *Broken Dreams: Vanity, Greed and the Souring of British Football* (Simon & Schuster, 2003)

Bravo, Lauren, *What Would the Spice Girls Do? How the Girl Power Generation Grew Up* (Bantam Press, 2018)

Brown, Adam and Walsh, Andy, *Not for Sale: Manchester United, Murdoch and the Defeat of BSkyB* (Mainstream, 1999)

Buckley, Andy and Burgess, Richard, *Blue Moon Rising: The Fall and Rise of Manchester City* (Milo Books, 2000)

Campbell, Alistair and Stott, Richard (eds.), *The Blair Years: Extracts from The Alistair Campbell Diaries* (Hutchinson, 2007)

Cantona, Eric, *My Notebook* (Weidenfeld & Nicolson, 2017)

Charlton, Jack, *Jack Charlton: The Autobiography* (Partridge Press, 1996)

Chidlow, David, *City 'Til I Die* (Polar Print, 1999)

Clarke, Stuart, *Football in Our Time: A Photographic Record of Our National Game* (Mainstream Publishing, 2003)

Clayton, David, *Kinkladze: the Perfect 10* (The Parrs Wood Press, 2004)

Clavane, Anthony, *A Yorkshire Tragedy: The Rise and Fall of a Sporting Powerhouse* (Riverrun, 2016); *Promised Land: A Northern Love Story* (Yellow Jersey Press, 2010)

Cohn, Nik, *Yes We Have No: Adventures in Other England* (Secker & Warburg, 1999)

Conn, David, *The Beautiful Game? Searching for the Soul of Football* (Yellow Jersey Press, 2005); *The Football Business: Fair Game in the 90s?* (Mainstream, 1997); *Richer Than God: Manchester City, Modern Football and Growing Up* (Quercus, 2012)

Couper, Niall, *This is Our Time: The AFC Wimbledon Story* (Cherry Red Books, 2012)

Cowley, Jason, *The Last Game: Love, Death and Football* (Simon & Schuster, 2009)

Cox, Michael, *The Mixer: The Story of Premier League Tactics, from Route One to False Nines* (HarperCollins, 2017); *Zonal Marking: The Making of Modern European Football* (HarperCollins, 2019)

David, Paul, *Liverpool Docks: A Short History* (Foothill Media, 2016)

Davies, Pete, *All Played Out: The Full Story of Italia '90* (William Heinemann, 1990)

Dempsey, Paul and Reilly, Kevan, *Big Money, Beautiful Game: Saving Football from Itself* (Nicholas Brealey Publishing, 1998)

Devlin, John, *True Colours: Football Kits from 1980 to the Present Day* (A&C Black Publications Limited, 2005)

Dobson, Stephen and Goddard, John, *The Economics of Football, Second Edition* (Cambridge University Press, 2011)

Dohren, Derek, *Ghost on the Wall: The Authorised Biography of Roy Evans* (Mainstream Publishing, 2004)

Du Noyer, Paul, *Liverpool Wondrous Place: From the Cavern to the Capital of Culture* (Virgin Books, 2007)

Evans, Tony, *Two Tribes: Liverpool, Everton and a City on the Brink* (Bantam Press, 2018)

Ferdinand, Les, *Sir Les: The Autobiography of Les Ferdinand* (Headline, 1997)

Ferguson, Alex, *Managing My Life: My Autobiography* (Hodder & Stoughton, 1999); *My Autobiography* (Hodder & Stoughton, 2013)

Ferris, Paul, *The Boy on the Shed* (Hodder & Stoughton, 2018)

Flight, Tom, *Yer Joking Aren't Ya? The Story of Middlesbrough FC's 1996/97 Season* (Pitch Publishing, 2020)

French, Ron and Smith, Ken, *Lost Shipyards of the Tyne* (Tyne Bridge Publishing, 2004)

Foot, John, *Calcio: A History of Italian Football* (Fourth Estate, 2006)

Fort, Patrick and Philippe, Jean, *Zidane: The Biography* (Ebury Press, 2018)

Fowler, Robbie with Maddock, David, *Fowler: My Autobiography* (Macmillan, 2005)

Fynn, Alex and Whitcher, Kevin, *Arsenal: The Making of a Modern Superclub* (Vision Sports Publishing, 2008)

Garton-Ash, Timothy, *History of the Present: Essays, Sketches and Despatches from Europe in the 1990s* (Allen Lane, 1999)

Gibbons, Michael, *When Football Came Home: England, the English and Euro 96* (Pitch Publishing, 2016)

Gibson, Keith and Booth, Albert, *The Buildings of Huddersfield: An Illustrated Architectural History* (Tempus Publishing, 2005)

Glanville, Brian, *The Story of the World Cup, Sixth Edition* (Faber & Faber Limited, 2001)

Goldblatt, David, *The Ball is Round: A Global History of Football* (Viking, 2006); *The Game of Our Lives: The Meaning and Making of English Football* (Viking, 2014)

Grant, Len, *Full Time at Maine Road* (Len Grant Photography, 2004)

Hamilton, Duncan, *Going to the Match: The Passion for Football* (Hodder & Stoughton, 2018); *Provided You Don't Kiss Me: 20 Years with Brian Clough* (Fourth Estate, 2007)

Hardy, Martin, *Touching Distance: Kevin Keegan, The Entertainers and Newcastle's Impossible Dream* (deCoubertin Books, 2015); *Tunnel of Love: Football, Fighting, Failure – Newcastle United After The Entertainers* (deCoubertin Books, 2016)

Harris, Daniel, *The Promised Land: Manchester United's Historic Treble* (Arena Sport, 2013)

Harris, John, *The Last Party: Britpop, Blair and the Demise of English Rock* (Fourth Estate, 2003)

Harris, Nick, *England, Their England: The Definitive Story of Foreign Footballers in the English Game Since 1888* (Pitch Publishing, 2003)

Haslam, Dave, *Manchester, England: The Story of Pop Cult City* (Fourth Estate, 1999)

Hatherley, Owen, *A Guide to the New Ruins of Great Britain* (Verso, 2012)

Hodgson, Alan, Thomas, Owen, Thomas, Ian and Ward, John, *99 Years and Counting: Stats and Stories – Huddersfield Town A.F.C. Centenary History* (Huddersfield Town Football Club, 2007)

Hodkinson, Mark, *Blue Moon: Down Among the Dead Men with Manchester City* (Mainstream Publishing, 1999)

Hornby, Nick, *Fever Pitch* (Victor Gollancz, 1992); *High Fidelity* (Victor Gollancz, 1995)

Hughes, Simon, *Allez, Allez: The Inside Story of the Resurgence of Liverpool FC, Champions of Europe 2019* (Bantam Press, 2019); *Men in White Suits: Liverpool FC in the 1990s – The Players' Stories* (Bantam Press, 2015); *On the Brink: A Journey Through English Football's North West* (deCoubertin Books, 2017); *There She Goes: Liverpool, A City on its Own – The Long Decade – 1979-1993* (deCoubertin Books, 2019)

Inglis, Simon, *Football Grounds of Britain, Third Edition* (Collins Willow, 1996); *The Football Grounds of Europe* (Willow Books, 1990)

Keane, Roy with Dunphy, Eamon, *Keane: The Autobiography* (Michael Joseph, 2002)

Keegan, Kevin, *My Autobiography* (Warner Books, 1997)

Keegan, Kevin with Taylor, Daniel, *My Life in Football* (Macmillan, 2018)

Kelly, Stephen F., *The Kop: Liverpool's Twelfth Man* (Virgin Books Ltd, 2008)

Keoghan, Jim, *Highs, Lows and Bakayokos: Everton in the 90s* (Pitch Publishing, 2016)

Kidd, Alan and Wyke, Terry (eds.), *Manchester: Making the Modern City* (Liverpool University Press, 2016)

King, Anthony, *The End of the Terraces: The Transformation of English Football in the 1990s* (Leicester University Press, 1998)

Kipling, Lesley and Brooke, Alan, *Huddersfield: A History and Celebration* (The Francis Firth Collection, 2005)

Kirklees Stadium: A New Concept in Sport and Entertainment (Kirklees Stadium Development Ltd.)

Kuper, Simon, *The Football Men: Up Close with the Giants of the Modern Game* (Simon & Schuster, 2011)

Kuper, Simon (ed.) *Perfect Pitch 1: Home Ground* (Headline, 1997)

Kuper, Simon and Araujo, Marcela Moray (eds.), *Perfect Pitch 3: Men and Women* (Headline, 1998)

Lake, Paul, *I'm Not Really Here* (Century, 2011)

Lansdowne, Greg, *Stuck on You: The Rise and Fall of Panini Stickers* (Pitch Publishing, 2015)

Lavalette, Michael and Kennedy, Jane, *Solidarity on the Waterfront: The Liverpool Lock Out of 1995/96* (Liver Press, 1996)

Lester, Sarah and Panter, Steve (eds.), *The Manchester Bomb From Devastation to Regeneration* (Manchester Evening News, 2006)

Lovejoy, Joe, *Glory, Goals and Greed: Twenty Years of the Premier League* (Mainstream, 2011)

Lyons, Andy and Ticher, Mike (eds.), *Back Home: How the World Watched France 98* (When Saturday Comes Books, 1998)

Malan, Colin, *The Magnificent Obsession: Keegan, Sir John Hall, Newcastle and Sixty Millions Pounds* (Bloomsbury, 1997)

Mallalieu, J.P.W., *Sporting Days* (The Sportsmans Book Club, 1957)

Marren, Brian, *We Shall Not be Moved: How Liverpool's Working Class Fought Redundancies, Closures and Cuts in the Age of Thatcher* (Manchester University Press, 2016)

Marshall, Tim, *Shadowplay: Behind the Lines & Under Fire – The Inside Story of Europe's Last War* (Elliott and Thompson Limited, 2019)

Mitten, Andy, *Glory, Glory! Man Utd in the 90s – the Players' Stories* (Vision Sports Publishing, 2009)

Moffat, Alistair and George, Rosie, *Tyneside: A History of Newcastle and Gateshead from Earliest Times* (Mainstream Publishing, 2005)

Neville, Gary, *Red: My Autobiography* (Bantam Press, 2011)

O'Neill, John-Paul, *Red Rebels: The Glazers and the FC Revolution* (Yellow Jersey Press, 2017)

Parlour, Ray with Lawrence, Amy, *The Romford Pele: It's Only Ray Parlour's Autobiography* (Century, 2016)

Paul, David, *Liverpool Docks: A Short History* (Fonthill Media, 2016)

Peace, David, *Red or Dead* (Faber & Faber, 2013)

Pearson, Harry, *The Far Corner: A Mazy Dribble Through North-East Football* (Little, Brown, 1994)

Platt, David, *Achieving the Goal; My Autobiography* (Richard Cohen Books, 1995)

Quinn, Niall, *The Autobiography* (Headline, 2003)

Rachel, Daniel, *Don't Look Back in Anger: The Rise & Fall of Cool Britannia, Told by Those Who Were There* (Trapeze, 2019)

Reade, Brian, *43 Years With the Same Bird: A Liverpudlian Love Affair* (Macmillan, 2008)

Rees, Paul, *When We Were Lions: Euro 96 and the Last British Summer* (Aurum Press, 2016)

Rich, Tim, *Caught Beneath the Landslide: Manchester City in the 1990s* (deCoubertin Books, 2018)

Rivoire, Xavier, *Arsene Wenger: The Biography* (Aurum Press Limited, 2007)

Robinson, Joshua and Clegg, Jonathan, *The Club: How the Premier League Became the Richest, Most Disruptive Business in Sport* (John Murray, 2018)

Rose, Ash, *Alive and Kicking: The Ultimate Book of 90s Football Nostalgia* (The History Press, 2013)

Ruddock, Neil with Smith, Dave, *Hell Razor: The Autobiography of Neil Ruddock* (CollinsWillow, 1999)

Ruhn, Christov (ed.), *Le Foot: The Legends of French Football* (Abacus, 2000)

Sampson, Kevin, *Extra Time: A Season in the Life of a Football Fan* (Yellow Jersey Press, 1998)

Scraton, Phil, *Hillsborough: The Truth* (Mainstream, updated 2016)

Sheard, Rod, *Sports Architecture* (Spon Press, 2001)

Shearer, Alan with Harrison, Dave, *Alan Shearer: My Story So Far* (Hodder & Stoughon, 1998)

Sinclair, Dave, *Dockers: The '95 to '98 Liverpool Lockout* (Amberley, 2015)

Spurling, Jon, *Highbury: The Story of Arsenal in N5* (Orion, 2006)

Storey, Daniel, *250 Days: Cantona's Kung Fu and the making of Manchester United* (HarperCollins, 2019); *Gazza in Italy* (HarperCollins, 2018)

Stubbs, David, *1996 and the End of History* (Repeater Books, 2016)

Szymanski, Stefan and Kuypers, Tim, *Winners and Losers: The Business Strategy of Football* (Viking, 1999)

Taylor, Rogan and Ward, Andrew, Newburn, Tim (eds.), *The Day of the Hillsborough Disaster: A Narrative Account* (Liverpool University Press, 1995)

The Alfred McAlpine Stadium: Fact Guide

Tucker, Richard, *End of an Era: Photo Memories of Manchester City at Maine Road* (Halsgrove, 2011)

Turner, Alwyn W., *A Classless Society: Britain in the 1990s* (Aurum Press Ltd., 2013)

Venables, Terry, *Born to Manage: The Autobiography* (Simon & Schuster, 2014)

Vialli, Gianluca and Marcotti, Gabriele, *The Italian Job: A Journey to the Heart of Two Great Footballing Cultures* (Bantam Press, 2006)

Walker, Michael, *Up There: The North East, Football, Boom and Bust* (deCoubertin Books, 2014)

Ward, Andrew and Williams, John, *Football Nation: Sixty Years of the Beautiful Game* (Bloomsbury, 2009)

Watson, Don, *Dancing in the Streets: Tales from World Cup City* (Victor Gollancz, 1994)

Whitcher, Kevin, *Gunning for the Double: The Story of Arsenal's 1997-98 Season* (Sporting Editons, 1998)

White, Jim, *Are You Watching, Liverpool? Manchester United and the 93/94 Double* (William Heinemann Ltd, 1994)

Whitworth, Tom, *Owls: Sheffield Wednesday Through the Modern Era* (Pitch Publishing, 2016)

Williams, David and de Kerbrech, Richard, *Glory Days: Swan Hunter* (Ian Allen Publishing, 2008)

Williams, John, *Red Men: Liverpool Football Club – The Biography* (Mainstream Publishing, 2010)

Williams, John, Hopkins, Stephen and Long, Cathy, *Passing Rhythms: Liverpool FC and the Transformation of Football* (Berg, 2001)

Wilson, Harold, *Memoirs: The Making of a Prime Minister – 1916-64* (George Weidenfeld & Nicolson and Michael Joseph, 1986)

Wilson, Jonathan, *Behind the Curtain: Travels in Eastern European Football* (Orion, 2006); *Inverting the Pyramid: The History of Football Tactics* (Orion, 2008); *The Anatomy of England: A History in Ten Matches* (Orion, 2010); *The Anatomy of Manchester United: A History in Ten Matches* (Orion, 2017); *The Anatomy of Liverpool: A History in Ten Matches* (Orion, 2013)

Winner, David, *Brilliant Orange: The Neurotic Genius of Dutch Football* (Bloomsbury, 2000)

Wright, Ian with Bradley, Lloyd, *Ian Wright: A Life in Football – My Autobiography* (Constable, 2016)

Reports/Journals

Deloitte & Touche: Annual Review of Finance (Various Years)

Dobson, Nigel, Holliday, Simon and Gratton, Chris, *Football Came Home: The Economic Impact of Euro '96* (The Leisure Industries Research Centre: Sheffield, 1997)

Hillsborough: The Report of the Hillsborough Independent Panel (HMSO, 2012)

Malcolm, Dominic, Jones, Ian and Waddington, Ivan, 'The people's game? Football spectatorship and demographic change', *Soccer & Society*, 1 (1), (2000)

The Hillsborough Stadium Disaster: Inquiry by Lord Justice Taylor – Interim Report (HMSO, 1989)

The Hillsborough Stadium Disaster: Inquiry by Lord Justice Taylor – Final Report (HMSO, 1990)

Williams, John, Perkins, Sean, *Ticket Pricing, Football Business, and 'Excluded' Football Fans: Research on the 'New Economics' of Football Match Attendance in England* (Sir Norman Chester Centre for Football Research, 1998)

Newspapers
The Chronicle (Newcastle)
Daily Express
Daily Mail
Daily Mirror
Daily Telegraph
Financial Times
The Guardian
Huddersfield Daily Examiner
The Independent
Liverpool Echo
London Evening Standard
Manchester Evening News
News of the World
The Observer
The Sun
Sunday Times
The Times

Magazines/Fanzines
The Blizzard
FourFourTwo
Loaded
Red Issue [Manchester United]
Toon Army News [Newcastle United]
True Faith [Newcastle United]
United We Stand [Manchester United]
Viz
When Saturday Comes

Websites
Football Ground Guide – footballgroundguide.com
Sporting Intelligence – sportingintelligence.com

Films (by director)
Boyle, Danny, *Trainspotting* (1996); *T2 Trainspotting* (2017)
Loach, Ken, *Looking for Eric* (2009)

Documentaries (by director(s))
Drummond, Challis and Wooster, David, *La Coupe de la Gloire: The Official Film of the 1998 FIFA World Cup* (1998)
Gordon, Douglas and Parreno, Philippe, *Zidane: A 21st Century Portrait* (2006)
Loach, Ken, *The Flickering Flame* (1996)
McGill, Ken, *An Impossible Job/Do I Not Like That* (1994)
Salles, Murili, *Two Billion Hearts: The Official Film of the 1994 FIFA World Cup (1995)*
Turner, Benjamin and Turner, Gabe, *The Class of '92* (2013)
Treharne, Jo, *Orient: Club for a Fiver* (1995)
Zimbalist, Jeff and Zimbalist Michael, *The Two Escobars* (2010)

Television
The Day Today (1994)
The Fast Show (1994-97)
Father Ted (1995-98)
Fantasy Football League (1994-98)
Football Italia / Gazzetta Football Italia (1992-2002)
Our Friends in the North (1996)

Podcasts
The Big Interview with Graham Hunter
Quickly Kevin, Will he Score? The 90s Football Show
Undr the Cosh

Other

Various VHS and DVDs, match programmes, club publications, Merlin and Panini sticker albums, and company accounts.

Kieran Maguire (of the Price of Football – priceoffootball. com) – Premier League financial statistics: 1992–present.

About the Author

Tom Whitworth is the author of *Owls: Sheffield Wednesday Through the Modern Era*. Previously he has written for *When Saturday Comes* and *FC Business* magazines. He lives in Sheffield, next to one of its five rivers.